TEACH ME
HOW TO LOVE

ABOUT THE AUTHOR

Malcolm S. Southwood is acclaimed internationally as a spiritual healer, lecturer, author, and teacher. He was born in England in 1940 and has a loving, supportive family, including four grown children.

During most of his professional life, Mr. Southwood was an agricultural businessman; and he was involved in agricultural business and management throughout the world.

Early in life, while working on large English estates, he began to observe the plant and animal kingdoms and to learn from them. Many of his teachings and healing techniques are inspired by his observations of nature.

Mr. Southwood discovered his healing gift in 1982 and has been practicing healing full time since 1983. He has traveled extensively and shared his universal wisdom, awareness, and healing energy with people of many nationalities and religions.

Dedicated to raising awareness and understanding of natural healing, Mr. Southwood is considered by many to be the world's foremost teacher and practitioner of Quantic Healing, harmonizing the body, mind, and spirit in perfect attitude, health, and awareness.

Mr. Southwood is the founder and director of The International Academy of Healing. His aims are to: return self-respect to those who have mislaid it; return independence to those who have lost it; and return love to those who have forgotten it.

TEACH ME HOW TO LOVE
So I Can Heal

Malcolm S. Southwood

THE INTERNATIONAL ACADEMY OF HEALING
West Chester, Pennsylvania

This book is sold subject to the condition that it shall not, by way of trade or otherwise, be lent, re-sold, hired out, photocopied, or held in any retrieval system, or otherwise circulated without the publisher's prior consent in any form of binding or cover other than that in which this is published and without a similar condition including this condition being imposed on the subsequent purchaser.

Copyright 1999 by Monument, Ltd.

First Edition
First Printing, 1999

Teach Me How To Love, Copyright 1999, by Malcolm S. Southwood. All rights reserved. Without limiting the rights under copyright reserved above, no part of this publication may be reproduced, stored in or introduced into a retrieval system, or transmitted, in any form or by any means (electronic, mechanical, photocopying, recording, or otherwise), without the prior written permission of both the copyright holder and the publisher of this book, except for brief reviews.

ISBN 1-893657-01-9

Published by
The International Academy of Healing
2012 Skiles Boulevard
West Chester, PA 19382-7304

Printed in the United States of America

*To Margaret, Debbie, Rosalie, and Jim,
without whom this book would not have lived;
and, of course, to Chrissies everywhere.*

My loving thanks.

The Cover Drawing

The symbol in the cover design was spiritually inspired and drawn by the author. It represents the universal love. Take the symbol into your thoughts and experience the inspiration of creative love.

Editing and Project Management:
James L. Walden, Ed.D.

Cover Photograph of the Author:
Nancy Burson

Cover & Book Design and Production:
Graphics Standard

Preface…ix

Introducing Chrissie …1

Love and Light…13

Purpose…21

Self-worth…29

Other Gods…35

To Kill Or Hurt…39

Forgiveness…49

Love Or Burden…57

Death and Dying...67

A Spiritual World...81

Love, To Be Or Destroy...95

To Live Or Die...111

Ability...121

Absent Healing...129

Spiritual Healing...139

Anger...149

Rejection...157

Guilt...165

Reincarnation...173

Fear...193

And Finally...203

PREFACE

My introduction to Chrissie was a bit of a surprise. I had been trying for several months to write about certain philosophies relating to emotion and what our lives are supposed to achieve; but somehow, the results were always heavy and anything but an interesting or entertaining read.

I have always believed that any book should, where possible, be entertaining as well as informative and interesting. The subject I was trying to write about didn't have much going for it as far as entertainment value was concerned. But the book was wanted. Many of my clients were asking me to commit to print the views I express during healing sessions.

On one memorable day, while attempting for the fifth time to start this book, I was staring at a blank sheet of paper when a voice distinctly said to me: "How about telling them my story?"

"What story is that?" I asked, not knowing who I had answered.

"Let me tell you about it," a youthful female voice replied.

"Don't you think you should introduce yourself first?" I suggested. "I need to know who I'm writing about."

I clearly heard her laugh, and then she appeared in my thoughts.

"Hi!" she said. "I'm Chrissie. I want to know all you can teach me; but first, write down what I'm about to tell you."

That is the absolute truth about how Chrissie and I were introduced. For the next six weeks, we went everywhere together. She asked me all kinds of questions and proved to be very argumentative at times, which she managed to get away with because of her beautiful sense of humor.

I'm afraid the following pages don't do justice to either Chrissie's personality or inquiring mind, but I have attempted to put some of our conversations down in writing. We hope you feel entertained as you read through the pages, even if you find some of the views unfamiliar to your thoughts.

With the exception of Chrissie, Debbie, my secretary, and myself, all other characters in the book are fictitious. The cases detailed herein were drawn from my personal experiences, gathered from many thousands of cases over a period of fifteen years. Should you think you recognize either a case history or a personality, I assure you it is pure coincidence. Chrissie and I have been most careful to use only fictitious names and situations.

*Lift the thought that you are Love
so high
that it drives fear out.*

– Malcolm S. Southwood

Chapter One
INTRODUCING CHRISSIE

Chrissie was young, beautiful, and artistic. Seemingly, she had everything to live for; but I could tell by her eyes that she was haunted by some fear of the past. I wasn't particularly busy the day Chrissie phoned up on the spur of the moment, prompted by some inner voice she told me later, and asked for an appointment.

"Can I come today?" she pleaded.

I had intended to put the day aside to write the sequel to my earlier book, *The Healing Experience*, but there was an urgency about her voice that caused me to think that seeing Chrissie was more important than writing a book.

"Okay, what's the problem?" I began, as she seated herself opposite me.

"I really don't know," she replied. "It's just that something is frightening me. It's not really an anxiety attack or anything as definite as that. It's not something that comes and goes. Malcolm, it's an underlying fear that seems to be following me around."

I sat back and let her continue.

"Life has been pretty good to me. I have kind, caring parents who have always been there when I needed them. I was born in the country near a small town where we own some land. I grew up in idyllic surroundings. I loved the woods, the fields, and the river that flows through our property; and I had lots of space to run, play, and feel free and safe."

My smile encouraged her to continue. "Later on, I left home to go to school. The high school was in beautiful surroundings, too, and I was lucky because learning was relatively easy. I was quite good at sports and most other school activities. My parents were supportive and we shared a good relationship."

Chrissie hesitated, as if waiting for me to respond. The silence was uncomfortable for her, so she began to tell me more about her life.

"After graduating from high school, I went on to a university to study art in all its forms. I'm really quite imaginative and find it easy to become one with whatever I'm creating. It's as if I move into another world whenever I get absorbed in my art. Anyway, to get to the point of why I'm here, life was fun with lots of friends and no responsibilities until I was twenty-three."

"How old are you now?" I interrupted.

"Nearly thirty-one. As I was saying, life was great until I was twenty-three. It was just after my twenty-third birthday that I met Byron. We were attracted to each other immediately. There was something about him...I couldn't get him out of my mind. I felt as if all my senses were conspiring to hand me to this man."

"Where did you meet Byron, Chrissie?"

"We met in a cafe in Philadelphia. He just happened to sit at my table. I was alone, and the place was full. The only spare chair was beside me. He didn't say anything—he just sat down."

I watched Chrissie's face as she spoke Byron's name and struggled with her emotions.

"Malcolm, it was really weird. I could actually feel his vibrations...like they were taking over me! Without his realizing it, he lifted me onto a totally different plane. All of my senses were heightened. Suddenly, I could hear every note of the music that was playing. I remember it exactly. The music was *The Celts*, by Enya. The coffee I was drinking had a caramel flavor, and the smell and taste of it were exquisite. My eyes took in everything about this man, who'd quietly sat down next to me. The room we were in, though really small, suddenly seemed large enough to hold the universe; and everything in it was a million miles away, except the music, the coffee, and the man next to me."

Her eyes closed for a moment, and I assumed that Chrissie was retrieving more details.

"Nothing in my life had prepared me for this. I was completely thrown. I became totally absorbed in his energy, feeling completely out of control. I knew I was in love—somehow afraid, but in love. I had been in love two or three times before, but this was different. I felt more than a physical attraction. The best way I can describe it is to say that it was like drowning in an ocean of energy, or like being lifted out of my body and into a state of euphoria. I was no longer a separate individual…I had become one with eternity."

"That was a powerful experience, Chrissie."

"Yes, Malcolm, it was. I was thinking that he must be about my age when he looked at me. Oh, those eyes! Then, he spoke and asked my name.

"Later, he told me that he was fascinated by me even though he already had a steady girlfriend. He said he didn't know what the fascination was, but he couldn't get me out of his mind after he left the cafe. I knew exactly how he felt."

"What happened after you left the restaurant?"

"I went home, and everything about our meeting kept going through my thoughts. Enya's music echoed in my mind as if it were the only song I'd ever heard, and I smelled caramel coffee everywhere I went. I didn't sleep that night—I just tossed and turned. Images of him—his eyes—filled my mind, and the music haunted me."

"This was an emotional encounter for you," I said to keep her talking.

"As for my emotions," Chrissie continued, "well, I don't know how to explain them. There was nothing sexual. I wasn't even sure I wanted to see him again. In fact, something at the back of my mind cautioned me not to, and I tried to forget him. But, that was out of the question. Early the next morning, after a sleepless night, I was organizing my day so that I would be at the cafe at the same time, hoping desperately that he would be there again, too."

"Please keep going, Chrissie. Tell me what happened."

"I knew that something, some force, was guiding my life and that I had no control of it. I was on automatic—in some sort of dream state. Like a zombie, I sat at the table and waited for him to join me. And, he did.

"I learned later that Byron had a similar experience, although his feelings and emotions weren't as intense as mine. As he put it, 'Against my better judgment, I found myself wanting to go back, hoping with half my mind to see you again while the other half hoped you wouldn't be there.'"

I overcame my urge to speak; and again, Chrissie broke the momentary silence.

"I suppose you've already guessed, Malcolm, that Byron and I soon became involved in an intense relationship. Strangely, I cannot say it was love. We couldn't stay away from each other; yet somehow, we didn't trust each other fully.

"Twelve months after we met, I was pregnant. I went crazy. I still can't explain the emotions I experienced at the time. I was terrified but didn't know why. Was it Byron? Was it me? Was it the baby? I didn't think it was the baby because I could quickly and easily have an abortion. I could not bring myself to tell him that I was pregnant, even though we were living together by this time. My world, my emotions, collapsed."

"Why were you so afraid, Chrissie?"

"I don't know. For some inexplicable reason, I was scared to tell Byron. He'd given me no reason to believe that he would be anything but understanding, but I kept putting it off."

"Did you ever tell him?"

"Yes, Malcolm, the time finally came when I couldn't put it off any longer. Byron had to be told. I couldn't figure out what was frightening me. After all, it was his baby; but I was consumed by an inner, unexplained fear. Telling him wasn't the traumatic experience I expected. When I told him, all he said was, 'Oh yes.' He hardly bothered to look at me when he added, 'What are you going to do about it?'"

"He gave me absolutely no reason to think that he was pleased, mad, sad, or anything else. I thought perhaps he hadn't heard me correctly. 'Byron, I'm pregnant,' I repeated. 'I know. You told me,' he said. I could feel myself shaking; and without thought, replied, 'I'm going to have an abortion.'"

Normally, during a consultation, I would have asked Chrissie to come to the point or moved her more quickly to it in some other way. However, I could sense all of this was important; and, anyway, I had the whole afternoon available. "What happened after the abortion?" I asked. "Did you go your separate ways?"

"Yes. Byron and I saw less of each other, and I moved back into my own apartment. We remained friends."

"Friends?"

"Just friends. I've dated some since, but I panic as soon as anyone tries to get close. An awful warning anxiety comes over me. This never happened before the abortion; but now, in any close relationship, I just want to run and hide."

"And what about Byron?"

"Byron has been quite good about it all. He's told me that he feels guilty—about my feelings, not the abortion. That's something he can't explain, either. Byron has tried other relationships with girls; but as soon as it starts getting into an emotional situation, he backs off."

I sensed that this part was still hurtful for Chrissie and waited for her to finish.

"We've tried to stop seeing each other totally, but this doesn't work, either. My life is a mess! It's been six years, and I'm nearly thirty-one. I have no possibility of ever having a steady relationship—never mind getting married!"

"So, Chrissie, what do you want me to do?"

"Please, Malcolm, can you get rid of this inner fear that follows me everywhere? My anxiety prevents me from having normal relationships with men. If you can, perhaps I will be able to get Byron off my mind. We still see each other and want each other at times, but we can't make a commitment."

"Okay, Chrissie, but a few questions first. Do you have any phobias?"

"Not that I can think of," she answered, giving the question a bit of thought.

"Any recurring dreams?"

"No, not really. I have the usual ones about falling. You know the sort of dream, I'm sure. The ones when you're falling into something that seems to have no bottom to it. In these dreams, I'm just falling and falling into nothing; but I haven't had one of these for a long time now."

"Do you have any aches or pains?" I continued.

"Well, I do actually; but I'm really more concerned with my emotional problems."

"I realize that," I said, "but spiritual healing is about healing the whole person—body, mind, and spirit; and I can't repair just this bit or that bit. I'll explain later how it works; but just for the moment, Chrissie, tell me about the physical problems."

"They're no big deal, Malcolm, really," she began. "I get a sharp pain that starts here in my right hip and goes down into my knee. Sometimes, the pain is worse in my knee; sometimes, it's in my hip. When the knee hurts, it feels as if it's being twisted."

"Have you seen a doctor about it?"

"Oh yes, several times. I've had every test imaginable, and the doctors say it's all in my mind. They may be right, but that doesn't make the aches any less. I've seen various alternative therapists also; and they told me there's nothing physically wrong. So, I just put up with the pain. Sometimes, it's very severe; and other times, I go for weeks and feel nothing."

"I think you've told me all I need to know at this stage, Chrissie. I just want you to sit in the chair and close your eyes. I'm going to let your subconscious take you back to the cause of your problems. Once you can identify with the cause, you can satisfy the emotion logically. By the way, do you believe in reincarnation?"

"In what?"

"You have heard about life after death?"

"Yes."

"Do you believe in it?"

"I haven't given it a lot of thought—life after death isn't part of my planning at the moment. Should it be?"

I smiled. I liked her sense of humor. "No, but I'm trying to assess if you can accept the notion that we have all lived before, perhaps many times, and that life, this life, is just one in a whole series of living experiences."

"At the moment, I'll believe anything that explains my fears and sorts my life out," she answered.

"Right, let's get on with it then."

Chrissie, eyes closed, began to relax. I had, while she was talking, already bonded with her energy vibrations. This is a relatively simple thing to do. We all radiate energy. The most powerfully radiated energy is emotional. That's the energy you feel when you walk into an argument and feel uneasy and out of place. We all radiate the energy vibrations of our thoughts. If our thoughts are hateful, vicious, or angry, we will drive away others whose thoughts are loving, gentle, and contented. This is a natural law. Similar energies attract each other, and energies of different frequencies repel one another.

The energy created by our thoughts is very powerful, indeed, and vibrates out into all time and space. Of course, the further it travels from the individual who created it, the weaker it becomes; but vibrations, once created, will follow their creators wherever they go until the thoughts are changed.

Chrissie's emotional energy was fear. I could feel and see it. It had a frequency and strength that was unique to Chrissie. In order to help her, I first needed to become one with that emotion. This doesn't mean that I also had to become fearful; rather, I had to take her fear into myself and remove all resistance.

This state is achieved by accepting unconditionally the person one is trying to help. To accept everything about them uncritically, just as they are, without any thoughts of wanting to change them.

Most people believe that healing, spiritual or otherwise, is about changing some aspect of a person's thinking, habits, or conditions in order to effect an improvement in their lives. Nothing could be further from the truth.

The first law of healing is to totally accept, unconditionally, the person who is asking for help. If a thought about causing a change in someone should cross my mind, even if it's what is logically being asked for, the effect would be to create a resistance in the mind of the one asking for help.

Their subconscious would pick up my thoughts of change and immediately create a wall of resistance. If people are going to change, they need to do it for themselves. Furthermore, to consider changing a person, I must have first considered the person to be imperfect. I must have judged them to be less than myself. This creates instant subconscious resistance.

I repeat, the first law of healing is total acceptance of a person for who they are at that point in time. This creates harmony. We are all different, all unique; and no one is more important than another. Everyone is special; and the ability to recognize the unique qualities, love, and pain of another without questioning them or wanting to change them allows one human being to harmonize with another.

I had harmonized with Chrissie. I had totally accepted her, without any thought of wanting to change her (even though that was why she had come to see me). If physical or emotional changes were going to happen in Chrissie's life, she was going to cause them. I was there just to help her into a state of greater awareness so that she could see more clearly the reasons for her difficulties and understand how to deal with them.

As the energies between us increased, I was able to lift Chrissie into an awareness state beyond and above logical perception. A vista opened in front of her, and she became one with emotions she had caused and been party to in a previous life. I stayed connected with her so that she could view her past. During the next forty minutes, she relived the experiences that were causing her so many problems in this life.

In her heightened state of awareness, Chrissie's first recall was of a scene similar to the one she had been brought up in. She found herself standing in a field looking across some water. She seemed perfectly relaxed and happy but was a bit puzzled about why she felt so cold. I knew her chill wasn't because of the room temperature because it was mid-summer, and, if anything, the room was a little warm.

"What are you wearing?" I asked her.

After thinking for a while, she answered, "...a heavy coat, woolly hat, gloves, and boots of some sort."

"Boots? Describe the boots, Chrissie."

She paused before answering, "I'm on ice; it's winter; I'm skating on the ice."

Suddenly, she had it all together. She could feel herself flowing across the ice, enjoying every minute of it. She described the scene and told me about other people who were skating with her. For some reason, which Chrissie wasn't absolutely sure about, she felt heavy and awkward; and, also, as the minutes went by, she sensed an emotion of anxiety rising in her. She told me later on that she also had a feeling of guilt that she couldn't place.

"What can you tell me about your anxiety?"

"Nothing much," she replied. "I'm just aware that it was there."

As she sat in the chair, her muscles began to tighten, as if she thought she might fall off. Chrissie began to sway from side to side, and her whole attitude changed from one of being reasonably relaxed to one of fear. I could feel her rising anxiety and hear it in her voice; and suddenly, she tightened her grip on the chair and let out a cry.

"I'm falling! I'm falling!" she shouted. In the same instant Chrissie lurched to the right; and her leg twisted back under the chair. She would certainly have fallen from the chair if I hadn't stopped her.

She was crying hysterically, "The baby, the baby. Have I hurt the baby?"

"What baby?"

"I'm pregnant," she cried. "He'll be mad at me. He told me not to come. Oh, my leg." She was moaning now as if in pain and holding her right leg.

"The pain in my leg…" she continued. "Oh the pain. It must be broken. I can't move—I can't get up. The baby…the baby."

Chrissie's emotions changed from the pain in her leg to fears about her unborn baby and back again. Her thoughts were in turmoil.

"What's happening now?" I asked.

"I'm being carried to a carriage."

As she was telling me this, she described a bit more of the scene and the people around her; and it became apparent that Chrissie had regressed to a previous life, sometime at the end of the Nineteenth Century.

She next recalled lying on a bed in a sparsely furnished room. She told me her leg was broken at the hip and that her knee was twisted and painful, but her main concern was for her baby.

She started to sob, "It's gone! I've lost it! I've lost my baby!"

At that moment, her body started to jerk from side to side.

"What's happening?" I asked.

"He's mad at me. He's in a rage. He's hitting me. He says it's my fault and that I did it on purpose to get rid of the baby; but I didn't. I didn't." she sobbed.

Chrissie's next recall was a few weeks later. She was still in obvious pain with her leg.

"He's still mad and won't speak to me," she cried; "and the pain in my leg is getting worse."

Chrissie felt hot and was scarlet red. She became hotter and hotter and told me she thought the heat was from an infection in her leg. Then, she was aware that a few days had passed and that her leg had been amputated. She told me now how her husband had rejected her. She felt lonely and unwanted.

"All because of that damned baby!" she shouted. Her attitude had changed to one of anger and bitterness, and she transferred all of the blame to the baby.

I asked her to move forward to the next trauma in her life, which was within a week or two. Apparently, infection set in after the operation; and she died in pain and fear soon afterwards.

Chrissie described how she felt herself lifting from the body and hovering above it for a few minutes before being drawn towards a light through some sort of tunnel. At this point, she opened her eyes.

"That was awesome," she said, after sitting quietly for a few minutes. "So many questions answered; so many mysteries solved. I expect you realize who my husband was in that life? He's Byron in this life, right?"

"How do you know Byron was your husband?"

"Oh, easily…by his eyes. There was something about my husband that was easily recognizable—nothing to do with his physical appearance, but something else. I saw something else in him. I have no doubt at all who he was. Everything fits. Now, I know why I'm so scared of getting into a relationship with a man and why I had to have the abortion. But why did I have to go through all of that? Was it really necessary, Malcolm? Was it a dream? Was I making it up?"

She paused for a moment before saying, "Oh yes, I forgot something when you asked me about phobias. I'm always very unsteady in icy conditions. I don't like icy weather at all and hate winter sports."

"You now have a lot of questions, Chrissie. Many of them will be answered in greater depth at another time, but I will give you some answers now so you will have some idea of what just happened."

"Oh, please," she said, "and I would like to come and see you again, to learn more."

"What you just experienced, Chrissie, was certainly no dream. We have all lived many, many times. I will give you the reason for this later; but for now, just understand that every emotion of every life you have experienced is still with you, or rather within your total personality profile. When the time is right, when you are ready to progress in your spiritual development—at a deeper spiritual level, I will help you to become free of the emotions that are holding you back. This can't be done until you make a spiritual decision to move away from material needs and the fears your emotions attract."

Chrissie was leaning forward and listening to every word.

"With help, I'm able to cast love around you, which makes it possible for you to face your fears and deal with them. This is what you have just experienced. You were full of unexplained fear—love helped to bring that fear to logical awareness, or to where you could deal with it in a logical way. If you had refused to accept this as fact, the fear would not have been dealt with, it would have returned to your subconscious, and your anxieties would have continued."

"That's certainly a lot to think about," Chrissie said. "I'm looking forward to deeper explanations of awareness. I'll call Debbie for an appointment."

Chapter Two
LOVE AND LIGHT

Chrissie phoned Debbie promptly and scheduled her second visit. Just seven days after her first appointment, Chrissie was seated opposite me in a more comfortable chair than the one she used during her regression.

"What's the problem this time?" I asked.

"Nothing at all," she replied, smiling. "I feel just great. All the unexplained fears have gone, and I feel like I used to, before I met Byron."

"Did you tell him about your past life?"

"Yes, but he just made fun of me. However, he did have to admit that I was looking radiant. He agreed that something had certainly changed, but he still thought the whole concept of reincarnation was a load of rubbish. 'When you're dead, you're dead! Phut, like a burned out light bulb, life ends!' was his expression."

"So, Chrissie, why are you here?"

"I want to know more—you've sparked my curiosity. I mean, if we really do have more than one life, what is the purpose of it all? Do we get richer and richer each time? Do we become more intellectual, though I don't think I would like that? How often do we come back? Are we always the same sex, or even species? I'm burning with curiosity."

I thought about her questions before answering. Not everybody is ready for this sort of information. Many people are still struggling with the concept of dealing with one life, and thoughts about dozens, or perhaps even over a hundred lives, might distress them further.

"What are your religious beliefs, Chrissie?"

"I was going to ask you that. To me, you sound like a Buddhist Jew with a Christian philosophy."

Smiling, I replied, "That's a funny concept. Where did you get that mixture?"

"I think the Buddhists believe we can become one with anything. I know the Jews have a belief in reincarnation, from bits I've read in a book called the *Kabbala*; and you talk a lot about love, which is a Christian doctrine. So, Malcolm, where do you stand on religious principles?"

This time, her question was direct, though not unfriendly. "I don't follow a specific religion, as such," I offered. "You see, it's not only the Christians who believe in love. Every religion is based on the love of the Supreme Being of their thoughts and teachings. The way each religion chooses to express its love, both within the laws the religion is founded on and within its community, causes the difference."

Chrissie was listening carefully, and I continued, "I believe every religion is about love, is built around love, and is the love of the Supreme Architect of awareness, or whatever name you choose to call the Great One."

"So, we're talking about Love?"

"Yes. If our lives are dedicated to serving Love, we must be prepared to serve each other because we are all creations of Love."

"Hmm...but what about your religion, Malcolm?"

"I have no specific religion, Chrissie. I serve them all. The moment we bind ourselves with laws and dogma, we set ourselves apart from the majority of Love's creations. To me, there is no such thing as a good religion or a bad religion. There are just different religions, and the differences between them gives us a more complete understanding of the supreme majesty of the ways of Love. The Supreme Being or Presence in everybody's life is Love."

I hesitated for a moment and allowed Chrissie time to process my remarks because they were foundations for the comments I was about to make. Her body language told me when she was ready to hear more; and I began by saying, "Before I was born, Chrissie, when I was still a spirit awaiting birth, Love spoke with me and said: 'I am giving you a great Love, as I give to all my children; but do not think it is yours, for you will not know of it until you give it away. I give you this Love in trust that you will use it wisely to satisfy the longing of any who should have need of it. Do not return to my keeping with any of the Love unused because it will be as stolen goods, and you cannot return to my keeping while you hold the Love meant for another.'"

"But what if I don't like this group or that group because of what they teach about you?" I asked Love.

"You shall not make judgments about My children; and so long as they share the Love that they are with all peoples, I will accept and Love them all," Love replied.

"That's very well," I thought under my breath, "but where do I get my Love from? If the Love I've been given isn't mine, where's mine?"

"The Love I grant to you I have placed in the hearts and souls of my other children."

I should have realized that even a thought is heard by the Creator of Love. "But what if I don't like these people, or religious groups?" I asked.

"Then you will have to go without my Love. I make no distinction between peoples or religions. If you turn away from any of my people, you turn away from my Love; and by that action, you turn away from me."

"Wow," sighed Chrissie, listening intently to every word. "Let me see if I got it. If we have been made a gift of God's Love, then we must all serve."

"That's just about the sum of it."

"But if Love isn't our own, and if we don't know we have it until we give it away, how can we possibly evaluate it? I mean...how do we give it away? We can hardly run around giving Love away like handing out dollar bills or candies, Malcolm. Just how are we supposed to give it away?"

"Love isn't like that," I replied, smiling. "You see, Love isn't what you *do*. Love is who you *are*. You are in effect open to everyone who wants to receive Love. The Love I talk about is the spirit, the divine spark inside every soul walking on Earth. Love is deep within us."

"I don't understand," mused Chrissie. "I see lots of people every day who claim to be very religious...always talking about God; but I can't honestly say I see a lot of Love shining from them."

"No, I'm afraid that much of the Love that we have has been fenced in with jealously, anger, fear, superiority, and other negative emotions."

I was about to move to another topic, but Chrissie hadn't finished with this one yet.

"Hang on a bit! You can't leave it like that!" she said sharply. "I want to know more about this Love. Is it the same love that I feel for a boyfriend, or a mother feels for her baby?"

"If the love you feel is unconditional, like a mother's love then, yes. But the instant you put conditions on it, it becomes emotional love, which is quite different from spiritual love."

I thought to myself, "Perhaps you shouldn't have started this conversation."

"Oh, I see," Chrissie chimed in, determined to understand what I meant by the term Love. "If it's not an emotion, then is it what you do for someone...like giving up your holiday to care for a sick friend...or letting someone get into your nice clean car on a wet day and soiling the seats, to save them a walk?"

"No Chrissie," I said slowly. "That's not the Love I'm talking about, either."

"Well, if it's not what you feel for someone, or not what you do for someone, what can it possibly be?" She was getting a little impatient. "Just saying I love you, or God loves you, without either sentiment or action, seems very shallow to my way of thinking."

"Alright, Chrissie, let me try to explain it another way. Imagine that this room we are in, with the light pouring through the windows, has big, heavy curtains on the inside and shutters on the outside. The room is full of people who are happy, laughing, friendly, and generally enjoying themselves."

"Ok. What about these people, Malcolm?"

"Now just suppose that someone decides to draw the curtains across the windows and to close the shutters on the outside. Within a few seconds, the room goes from being brightly lit to total darkness. What sort of effect do you think the change in light would have on the people and the party? How do you think the people would feel or react?"

"I suppose they would get very quiet," she reasoned. "No one would dare to move in case they knocked something or someone over or hurt themselves."

"They would certainly stop enjoying themselves, Chrissie. Most everyone in the room would become a little bit afraid. I expect they would become scared of each other because the light had gone, and they would have to concentrate on themselves instead of each other. Right?"

"…seems logical."

"And how do you think the people would feel if the curtains and shutters were parted and light again poured into the room?"

"I think they would relax again and notice what other people were doing," she said.

"And what has the light done, Chrissie?"

She thought for a moment before answering. "The light hasn't done anything, I suppose," she said slowly. "It's just there."

"Exactly," I agreed. "Light and Love in this context are the same, interchangeable. The Love I talk about makes you feel good just because it's there. It doesn't do anything. You can't feel it; but when it shines into your life, it acts as inspiration, and removes fear. Chrissie didn't reply, so I reiterated my point. "Some people have the same effect. Just because they are in our world, we feel better, more at peace with ourselves, softer. Such people don't necessarily do anything or say anything, but they give others inspiration to act, to lose fear, and to be Love."

I looked deeply into Chrissie's eyes and said, "Love is not something you *do*. It is something you *are*."

"Is this Love God?" Chrissie questioned.

"Yes, God doesn't do anything. God, the Supreme Loving Awareness, just is. Once you have removed the emotions that act as curtains, preventing the light from entering your life, your whole world will change. What you see, feel, or experience will remain unchanged, in a logical sense; but your awareness will change. The Love I speak of will change your sense of contentment and happiness; and others will change their perceptions of you and their feelings about you. This Love changes you on the inside."

"Hmm," she sighed.

"You see," Chrissie, "becoming Love is not something you do for your own good. Remember, you can't know your own Love. Becoming Love is a matter of what that love does for others. The love that you do or feel is physical or emotional. The Love we're talking about causes others to release their Love for you. The Love we enjoy comes from those around us. By changing to become Love, we begin to appreciate the Love around us, the Love that is for us."

Chrissie had become very quiet.

"How do we become that Love? Please tell me, Malcolm."

"Free yourself from negative emotions, Chrissie, and watch the world around you change."

"You'd make a good politician," she replied, smiling.

"Why do you say that?"

"We started this consultation off with my asking about reincarnation, and you neatly turned the discussion around to Love and Light. You haven't answered my question about reincarnation at all."

"We'll talk about that subject another time, Chrissie, I promise you. Love can be learned only through the many experiences of life. Before we go on an excursion into the spiritual spheres, I want you to know all about the Love you *are* in this life."

Chapter Three
PURPOSE

"Malcolm?"

Chrissie's voice was on the telephone.

"Would you do something for me, Malcolm?"

"If I can."

"I have a friend who was involved in a car accident three years ago and is very depressed. I won't go into the details, but she was hit by a drunk driver. The accident would not have been as serious if she had been wearing a seat belt, but she wasn't. Somehow, Jane was thrown between the front seats, and her spine was severed. She has been in a wheelchair ever since. I've told her you will see her. You will…won't you, Malcolm?"

"You know I will, Chrissie. Will you be present?"

"No, but her husband will be there. He's a wonderful man and has given up everything to care for her. She is paralyzed from the chest down and unable to do much for herself, which is why she's depressed."

Chrissie gave me Jane's address and made an appointment for me to visit her the following week. Such visits are always difficult the first time because everyone hopes for a miracle cure. Miracles do happen; but in most cases, healing has to begin on the inside. So, in all healing situations, I have a completely open mind and no preconceived ideas about what will be. My purpose, if I have one is to let those I'm visiting decide how the energies of healing love can best be utilized. Life is about the way we think—not about what we can do or not do.

Jed opened the door, and I could see immediately how this tragedy had affected every area of their lives. I had noticed the ramp up the steps and the van in the driveway that had been converted for wheelchair access. Entering the house, my eyes were drawn to the doorways that had been widened, the chair lift on the stairs, and the other alterations necessary to accommodate a wheelchair. Jane was waiting, and Jed introduced us right away.

"Coffee or soda?" Jed asked.

"No thanks," I replied. Especially not coffee. It's the last drink a healer needs before working. In fact, I neither eat nor drink, except water, while I'm giving healing."

"Why's that?" Jane asked, looking puzzled. "Surely, you need to eat something midday?"

"Perhaps just an apple and a glass of water. Anything heavy would just sit in my stomach until evening. While I'm working, most of my energy is utilized lifting me to a higher level of vibrations, as well as harmonizing with patients; so it isn't going to be used very much for digesting food."

"Well surely a drink wouldn't hurt you," Jed shouted from the hallway.

"It's easier to go without," I responded. "Water is usually too cold and just lies there, soda is too gassy, and coffee, of course, is a stimulant; and I'm trying to settle emotions—not stir them up. In fact, taking a client into the healing state of awareness can be quite difficult if they've had a coffee, or two, before coming to see me.'

Jed now joined us in the front room. Initially, he was very unsure about having a 'healer' in the house; but the chat was easy and friendly. He began to relax.

"So, Malcolm, what are you going to do with my wife?" he chuckled. "Hypnotize her, or something?"

Jed and Jane smiled at each other, and I could see they were taking the whole situation in a very relaxed manner, which was as it should be.

"Just relax, Jane; be open minded…anything but serious," I suggested.

When Jane began to explain the circumstances that led to her being bound to a wheelchair, Jed excused himself, explaining that he and Jane had agreed that it would be better if I saw Jane alone. He understood that Jane wanted to express thoughts and feelings that she couldn't release easily in his presence.

Once we were alone, I encouraged Jane by saying, "Ok, Jane, tell me all about it."

Soon, the healing energy helped her to release the hopelessness she felt about her injuries. She burst into tears, which is a common reaction. A healing presence will often cause a release of tension and unhappiness. I waited until she had finished and regained her composure.

"I feel so useless," Jane told me. "My life has no purpose; I'm just in the way. Jed is wonderful, but he could do so much more…if I didn't hold him back."

"Why do you have to have a purpose?"

"Everyone has to have a purpose in their life," she replied, "or life is meaningless."

"Rather depends on how you view the word *purpose*, Jane."

"What do you mean, Malcolm?"

"Jane, have you ever stopped to think about the oak tree, or any tree? Think for a moment about how magnificent oak trees are in the fall. Recall the wondrous colors of their leaves. Now, Jane, do you know that these trees really couldn't care less whether you notice them or not?"

"Hmm," she sighed, agreeing.

"It's the same in the spring when warmth returns life to the skeletons of trees and bushes in the form of unfurling leaves and fruit buds. The fresh greenery of spring is incredible! But trees are not interested in whether you appreciate them or not."

"That's right," Jane said softly.

"Furthermore, trees are home to millions of lives. Their leaves provide shelter from sun and rain; their bark protects from the harshness of winter. Each tree is a universe, observing life and death every day as old life makes way for new life. All of this goes on in the world of a tree, but the tree really isn't interested. A tree has no purpose. In the whole of its lifetime, a tree doesn't go anywhere or do anything. It just stays in the same place, doing nothing. It has no purpose to fulfill. It doesn't agonize about being a home to birds and insects or fulfilling a purpose. A tree just is! The only interest a tree has is to enjoy the beauty of life around it…feeling the air breeze through its leaves on a hot summer day…hearing the gentle bounce of its fruit, as the tree returns its soul to the earth."

"That's beautiful, Malcolm," Jane said.

"Right, Jane. Trees don't alter their shape or the size of their leaves; they don't try to accommodate more life by being more acceptable or of more value to others. A tree accepts itself for what it is—as it is. If it suits others to use it, that's fine with the tree. If others don't like it, that is still alright with the tree. A tree has no purpose, Jane. Other lives make the tree their purpose."

"What about other life?"

"The same is true with the birds in the sky, Jane. They have no purpose—nothing to achieve. Birds don't worry about flying higher than other birds or achieving some objective in some soon-to-be-forgotten future. They live to enjoy the beauty of awareness, to experience life in all its different shades."

"Nature is so lucky to have such freedom," Jane thought aloud.

"Freedom of purpose…fish don't worry about getting from here to there. Some crawl, some swim, and some float. But they have no purpose except to enjoy the beauty around them. We are just like trees, birds, and fish, and all other life in nature. We have no purpose except to enjoy the love and beauty that fills our lives."

The lines in Jane's brow deepened as she processed these thoughts. I disturbed the momentary silence by adding, "Like all others, I have no real purpose; but if we do have some purpose, others have chosen it for us by appreciating who we are in our life."

"How can you possibly say that you have no purpose!" she interrupted. "Yours is to heal and to bring peace and happiness into people's lives."

"No, Jane, you are quite wrong. I heal only because I can and because people ask me to, but it's not important. If people stop asking, I will do something else. My purpose in life comes from the people around me…from their love…from their happiness…from their beauty. My purpose, if I have one, Jane, is to appreciate what others do naturally with their love."

I paused. Jane obviously needed some time to absorb these thoughts. When she looked up and made eye contact, I said, "If I spent a day sitting in the sun watching the sea and some insect or little animal used my shadow to protect itself, my purpose was not to protect them from the sun—they made me their purpose. You, Jane, are no different. Your purpose, if you have one at all, is to appreciate the love and beauty of the friends and life around you. Can't you understand how special you are…just because you are alive. No one is important, but everyone is special. Every life, of every type, is special, just because it's there."

"But…"

"In this moment that you and I are together, Jane, you are the most special person in the world to me. In this instant, in this second, no one else exists—there's just you and me. To appreciate the beauty you are is my purpose. Your wonderful husband, who's now outside the house, is looking at other life, flowers, trees, your pets; and they will be his purpose as he enjoys the beauty and love of the life around him. As the birds, insects, and trees enjoy his caring, loving ways, he will become their purpose.

"I want to believe you, Malcolm."

"We don't live to have purpose for others, Jane. Others, if

they choose, and have love in their hearts, make us their purpose; and we see purpose in others just because they are there. We cannot know what others want or need. We can only be ourselves, fulfilling whatever dreams we have from the situation we have been given…just like a tree."

"I just don't feel very special, now that I'm confined to this wheelchair."

"Remember, Jane, you are special to every person who comes into this room to be with you. While with you, you are the most special person in their life in that instant of time. If you were not of this world, all of our lives would be less…because you glow with the light of God's Love. Because you are here, I know He still loves the world, just as I know he still loves the world when I watch birds and see autumn colors on trees."

"It's hard for me to believe that I fulfill any purpose, now, Malcolm."

"Jane, understand, we make the world our purpose; and in loving and appreciating it, we become part of that purpose. You are fulfilling your purpose just because you are here."

"But I could do so much more if I could walk—if I could be like other people."

"You're changing the subject, Jane."

"What do you mean?" she asked sincerely.

"Come on, Jane, think about it. You are comparing yourself to other people."

"Well, of course I am," she replied. "Others can walk and run; I can't. Is it so wrong to want to be like others?"

"I see," I said. "Let's think about this. What's really getting to you is that you want to be the same as everyone else."

"Of course."

"And it's because they can walk and you can't that you feel somehow cheated, incomplete?"

"Yes."

"So how would you feel if no one could walk and everyone had to use a wheelchair?"

A long silence followed my question. When Jane looked at me, I said: "Look Jane, if everyone in the world had wings and could fly, except me, I suppose I would feel cheated, somehow less than perfect. But because no one else can fly, I don't worry about it. That argument is just as silly as yours. If I felt unhappy five minutes ago because I thought others could fly, why am I now feeling happy because I've just realized they can't? I should really be basing my sentiments on what I can do—not what others can or cannot do. If I'm going to spend all my life comparing my various abilities with others, it's going to be a pretty miserable experience. There is so much that others do that I can't. Some people have wonderful voices; others grow beautiful flowers. I have friends who are fantastic with figures. I can't do any of these things!"

"Perhaps I have been too focused on my physical limitations," Jane admitted.

"The moment we begin to concentrate on what we can't do, our lives fall apart. There will always be more we can't do than things we can do; and then, the only way to retain our self-respect is to find fault with other people."

"I understand what you're saying. I just don't know how to apply it, Malcolm."

"What were you good at before your accident?"

"You mean apart from dancing and hill climbing?" she asked, smiling. She was being facetious but was, in fact, finding her sense of fun again. "I love my garden and am quite a respectable artist."

Jed knocked on the door and said, "How are you two getting on?"

"Malcolm's just told me what I need to be my old self again," Jane replied, laughing.

"Oh yes, what's that?"

"He says I need to concentrate on what I can do, not what I used to do. So, Jed, will you buy me some equipment?"

"If it will change your life and make you happy again, of course I will."

I winced. I could see what Jed was letting himself in for. "I'll let myself out," I suggested. However, Jed insisted on seeing me to the door. As I looked back, Jane waved goodbye and gave me a broad wink from behind his back.

"Thanks for coming," Jed said, shaking my hand.

Chapter Four
SELF-WORTH

I just knew it was Chrissie. The phone had that it's-me-again tone about it. "Hi Chrissie," I said, speaking before she said anything. She was so full of something to say that she didn't even notice I hadn't asked who was calling.

"I spoke with Jane last night," she told me.

"How is she?"

"Fantastic…got all sorts of ideas and plans. Jed is not so sure about you though."

"Wait for it," I thought.

Chrissie rattled on. "Says you've let him in for some expensive investments, but he doesn't really mind."

"How's that?"

"Well, to start with, there's the new greenhouse that Jane wants. She's already written several letters asking for catalogues, and now she deciding what type of plants to specialize in."

"I'm pleased that she's gotten so involved in a new interest. I'm sure Jed won't object to the cost."

"Oh, Malcolm, it's not just the greenhouse," Chrissie went on. "Jane wants an art studio built as well. I wouldn't be surprised if he sends you the bill for that one!"

"Ok, Chrissie, when do you want to see me?"

Next day, Chrissie was in the office.

"Can I ask a question about what you and Jane discussed? She said you told her, 'Once we compare ourselves to others, we start to find faults with them.' What did you mean by that?"

"Well, Chrissie, it's a complex problem; and, unfortunately, all of the world seems to be caught up in it."

Chrissie settled into her chair and looked at me as if to say, "Go on."

"For some strange reason, people count or value their worth by what others have, including anything like fine houses, great wealth, artistic talent, or good health. The list is endless, and people compare what they don't have with what others do have."

"How does this relate to my question, Malcolm?"

"This, of course, causes great problems for a person's ego or self-worth. People tend to turn the whole thing around; and instead of valuing or appreciating what others have, they look for what they don't have, trying to make themselves feel good."

"That's a bit complicated, Malcolm. Are you trying to tell me that in order to avoid being envious or jealous I should be critical or superior in some way?"

"No, not at all; but that's exactly what happens."

"You'd better explain this again," Chrissie suggested.

"You see, Chrissie, jealousy and envy are hurtful. They cause you to think you are inferior in some way, through ability, social standing, wealth, and many other ways. We have all been taught that both envy and jealousy are wrong. So, people tend to ignore the good, the advantages others have, and look for faults instead. And, of course, everyone is lacking something. This way, people make themselves feel better."

"You really mean it, don't you?" Chrissie asked, looking astonished. "…that people look for faults in others in order to make themselves feel better."

"Yes, Chrissie, I do. The peoples of the world have become super critical as a way of maintaining their self-worth—all because they compare themselves with others. Nations find fault with nations; religions find fault with other religions. Friends find fault with friends; and if you doubt, listen to people's conversations. Many conversations are made up of negative comments about others."

"I'm not sure...Malcolm."

"Think about it, Chrissie. Parents find fault with other children and try to make their own appear better. Religions find fault with other religions and believe that God prefers them and their practices. The media is full of criticism of situations, products, and people. The horrible truth is that people don't like to hear someone else being praised or put into a better light than themselves."

"Oh! I don't believe that!" Chrissie snapped.

I smiled to myself—I'd touched a raw nerve. "Alright," I said, "prove me wrong. For the rest of this week, go around praising people to others. Praise their work, their religion, their appearance, or whatever makes someone feel good. Talk about someone else who is just as good. Comment on how clever other people's children are, especially if someone is praising their own. Or, mention what a great healer someone is to friends who believe they are great healers, but perhaps of a different belief system. Believe me, Chrissie, people won't like your comments; and by the end of the week, you'll have fewer friends."

"This is nonsense!" Chrissie was getting really agitated now. "I have lots of friends, and they are lovely people who would do anything for anyone, who never say a bad word about anyone."

"I agree. There are a few saints about; but for one week, just try what I've suggested."

"You mean I've got to go out and deliberately offend people?" she asked.

"...not very tactful, is it?" I sensed that Chrissie was beginning to get the point.

"Why?" I kept the pressure up.

"Well," she hesitated. "They will feel put down. For example," she said with a flourish, as if she had just discovered the equation to life, "if I tell my friend Ken, who thinks he's a whiz with computers, how brilliant John is with computers, my comment will upset his ego."

"How do you think Ken will respond?"

"I know exactly how he will respond!" she went on, without stopping to think of the consequences of her answer. "He'll say…" She stopped abruptly when her thoughts caught up with her voice.

"Well?"

"It doesn't matter, but he'll probably make some sarcastic comment about what a jerk John is with computers—how he only plays with them in his business."

"You see what I mean?"

"So how are you going to change all this, Malcolm?"

"I can't change anything, Chrissie. Too many people are trying to change the world, thinking they are making it better. Unfortunately, most everyone thinks that other people need to change. Anyway, I don't particularly want to change anyone or anything. My advice is to accept everyone as they are. See the love in everyone, and perhaps they will change themselves, if they want to. Only an individual can know what is best for self."

"There you go," Chrissie interrupted. "You changed the conversation again."

"I didn't."

"Yes you did!" she insisted. "One minute, we were talking about 'being critical'; and in the next sentence, you were going on about changing the world."

"Alright, then, let's wind up this conversation on how we value ourselves and others."

Chrissie nodded, as if to acknowledge that she had scored a point.

"Here are four principles to consider, Chrissie:

1. It's not a fault to be without a gift that another might have.

2. We should be pleased that others have gifts we don't have. Otherwise, our world would be a boring, drab sort of place. Can you imagine everyone being an artist, good artists, and no one being good at making paints? What if everyone was good at making money—everyone had lots of money, but no one was good at making things to spend it on.

3. Let's stop comparing ourselves to others. Be pleased others are different…have what we don't have…can do what we can't do. By doing so, we can count their gifts as our own.

4. Make others the enjoyment and contentment in our life by praising what they do well. Feel the joy of helping others feel really good about themselves."

"Do you really think people can live by these principles?" Chrissie asked, speaking sincerely.

"You will be able to do this only when you are content with your own state of Love. It always comes back to the question, 'Can you accept yourself?' If the answer is 'Yes,' great, then help others accept themselves as they are. If the answer is 'No,' then do something about it; but don't find faults in others to hide your own imperfections."

"Do I do that?" Chrissie asked.

"Don't be silly, Chrissie. You know I didn't mean you. The next time you hear someone criticizing another, ask yourself what they are trying to hide in themselves. If you catch yourself judging another, ask yourself what gifts they have that you don't have."

"You make it sound so easy, Malcolm."

"You know, Chrissie, the world would be a great, happy, contented place if people counted the blessings others have, if people were grateful that someone possesses what they lack."

"Why do you turn everything upside down?"

Chrissie wasn't really expecting an answer, but I gave her one anyway. "Well, Chrissie, I find that the truth is usually at the bottom of the list of alternatives. So, why not start there?"

Chapter Five
OTHER GODS

"Morning, Debbie!"

"Hi! Boss."

"It's a great day out there."

"It's the same day in here," she said, laughing.

This bundle of fun held the positions of secretary, travel agent, coffee maid, and a whole collection of others too numerous to mention.

"You've got a visitor in the reading room."

"This early in the morning? Who is it? No, don't tell me. Let me guess. It's Chrissie."

Debbie's laugh said, "You got it."

I went to the room that was set aside for people who wanted to sit quietly after a healing treatment. "Hi, Chrissie. Would you like to come and sit with me while I go through the mail?"

As she followed me into my room, I realized that she was strangely quiet. What's wrong?" I asked.

"Oh, it's nothing you can do anything about, Malcolm. I have a friend who is about to have her house repossessed."

"What's gone wrong?"

"You don't know her, but my friend had to have some emergency medical treatment after an accident. There didn't seem to be a problem at the time. She had insurance, and the hospital and the doctors went ahead with the operations and treatments. Then, when it was all over, the insurance company found some legal loophole that allowed them to avoid payment of her expenses. Now, the two doctors are demanding payment."

"How long have they given her?"

"She's already had five years and has been trying to pay it off in installments. However, the courts have finally decided against her, and they're demanding payment in a few weeks."

"This must be stressful for her."

"Yes, everyone involved knows that she can't possibly raise the money, so a lien was filed on her house. She's nearly out of time."

"Doesn't she have any friends who could help?"

"Yes, but you know how it is. She won't ask, and they're full of empty sympathy. Why are people so selfish? It's not as if they really need the money—they have big cars, big houses."

"Hold on, Chrissie. You're judging people."

She was really unhappy this morning, and I realized that she was disturbed by the plight of her friend.

"Of course I'm judging people!" she exploded. "Is that also wrong? You know I don't think I like this Love thing of yours, Malcolm. It provides excuses for people who won't help and protects those who don't care if they take someone's home—just to add to their pot of gold."

"The problem, Chrissie, is that they have a different god than ours. We pray to our God of Love and live by the rules of Love. The people you don't like this morning pray to different gods; and, therefore, they live by different rules, so that makes them feel ok."

"How can they possibly pray to a different god?" she asked, looking somewhat surprised at the suggestion. "They're not heathens—they pray to our God the same as we do."

"They might say they do, but in their hearts, they pray to the gods of wealth and power."

She was listening intently for my next remark. "You see, Chrissie, their gods of wealth and power cheat."

She smiled and said, "Cheat! Oh, come on Malcolm. How can gods cheat?"

"Easily. Our God of Love gives us all we need or want in the little we have, and it always seems to be a lot because it comes parceled in Love. We are content with the little we have because our lives are full of Love."

"Keep going, Malcolm. I'm wondering where you're headed."

"Those who worship the gods of riches and power are rewarded with riches and power, and they see no reason why they should share with anyone else. Material wealth and power is, after all, their reward for being true to their gods."

"But how is that cheating?" she thought aloud.

"Because these gods don't tell their followers that there's a price to pay. The price they pay to have wealth and power is to give back the love they held in trust for others; so when they return to the spiritual world, they will realize that they're bankrupt of Love and beauty. You see, Chrissie, you can't serve two masters …you can't serve Love and greed. Some choose greed over Love, out of fear and insecurity, and so become spiritually bankrupt."

"But I expect our God will take pity on them and give them a new account," she said, revealing a tinge of sarcasm.

"You've forgotten what I told you earlier, Chrissie."

"What?"

"Love isn't something you *do* or can give away. It's who you *are*, and if you have forfeited that Love to make way for material or emotional wealth…"

"What's emotional wealth?" she interrupted.

"Power, fame, physical and emotional abuse, perversions …it's those sorts of things."

"Oh, I see."

"As I was saying…"

"Sorry."

"If you forfeit Love to have more than you need, by taking from others when their need is greater than yours, you will have destroyed something of yourself more precious than any material bounty. You will have destroyed your gift of Love; and when the time comes that you need it, you won't have it. Neither will those who are Love be able to give you theirs—no matter how much they want to. Love is the only protection against hurt, which we have and I wouldn't want to live without it, or leave this world without it."

"That's all very well, Malcolm, but it's not going to help my friend keep her house. Is it?"

Chrissie had a point. She was always practical. "No, it probably won't, but something will take its place. Love doesn't replace houses with houses, but it provides a deep inner peace and contentment, which sustains you through adversity and difficulties until things come right again. And, they always do."

I gave Chrissie time to process our discussion about other Gods. I knew that she was relating the information to her friend's situation. When she nodded, I said: "I'm not trying to make excuses for those who are destroying homes and happiness with insatiable greed, but until this Love thing, as you called it, spreads, the greedy will have their way."

"Right!"

"As long as your friend keeps her trust and faith in Love, everything will eventually come right; but if she becomes vindictive or loses faith, she will be giving up the one and only way to happiness."

Chrisse was silent for a moment and then got up to leave.

"Where are you going?"

"Well, I can't give my friend the money she needs, but I can bring happiness to the surface with Love and caring. She needs friends now—not my anger."

"Chrissie looked happier when she left," Debbie commented. "What did you say?"

"Nothing, she just replaced the anger she felt with Love."

Chapter Six
TO KILL OR HURT

"Do you think it's wrong, Malcolm, to kill?"

"Why? Who has annoyed you this time?"

"No, I'm serious, Malcolm."

"Chrissie, today is a beautiful day. The sun is shining, and I can hear children playing outside. Why do you want to spoil the day by asking me to be serious and talk about killing?"

"I know. You're right," she conceded, "but I asked the question because I can hear the children playing and laughing."

We were having what had now become regular discussion sessions. Sometimes in the office; sometimes on the beach. On this occasion, Chrissie invited some friends to join us, and I sensed the topic would arouse a lot of passion."

"Let's go on the beach," I suggested. "We're going to need a breeze blowing though this conversation to keep it light!"

We all moved down to the beach and sat on some rocks that stretched into the ocean. "Now, Chrissie, what's the point of your question?"

"I've been thinking about something you said earlier," she started. "You know, a few weeks ago, you said that we should not withhold Love from anyone. You said that Love is who we *are* …that negative emotions of anger, and all that stuff, only hurt us."

"Yes, I remember."

"Well, Malcolm, I'm having trouble accepting all of this."

"Why?"

"Oh, come on, Malcolm, get real! Are you trying to tell us that we have to love people like the Oklahoma bombers, who killed and maimed children? Or, do we have to be Love to other terrorists who deliberately destroy the lives and happiness of innocent people for some crazy personal ideology? Be serious!"

I sensed that Chrissie's remarks expressed more than just her sentiments. Her friends felt the same. "Remember, I told you that Love, spiritual Love, is like light. This Love is not an emotion or something we *do*; it's something we *are*."

Chrissie answered with a slow "Yes."

She didn't want to agree to any part of this conversation "...and do you agree that light is nonselective—that it shines on everyone equally?"

No one answered.

"Spiritual Love is just the same. If you allow your spiritual Love, which is your real awareness, to shine through, you cannot cause it to shine on this one but not that one. Spiritual Love is for everybody. Love is who you *are*. You cannot look pretty for me and ugly for someone else."

"But I could…"

"No, Chrissie. The Love you have isn't yours. You don't even know of it until you see it reflected in the eyes of those around you and if you're going to try and withhold that Love from this one or that one, you will have to withdraw it from everybody. You will have to change your character."

"I still have difficulty thinking that I've got to love a child killer," Chrissie persisted, without looking at me as she said it. One or two others shuffled on the rocks, expressing their agreement.

"You haven't fully understood what I mean by *being* Love."

"As long as we don't have to tell psychotics we Love them, and keep our feelings to ourselves, I suppose I could ignore them," one of Chrissie's friends said.

"But you don't even think about it." I was having difficulty with this one. "This Love is who you *are*. It's what you feel…totally without anger towards anyone."

"That's even worse!" Chrissie said, shrugging her shoulder and sighing deeply. "You mean I can't even be angry when a child is killed?"

I watched as she worked her frustration out on a poor little crab in the rocks, poking at it with her fingers. "There is nothing wrong with being angry, Chrissie. Anger can be a reaction to danger or hurt—an instinctive reaction to keep you safe. The problem starts if you allow yourself to *become* anger."

I paused to encourage Chrissie and the others to give my last comment some thought. "One is just a *passing* phase and doesn't affect the Love that shines from you. The other *replaces* the Love so that anger becomes who you *are*."

An audible sense of relief swept through the group as their imaginations caught the comparison between Love and anger.

"Ok," Chrissie said, giving the crab a few moments of respite. "Now I think I've got it. What I think you're saying," she went on, "is that I may feel passing anger, even outrage at what mindless people do; however, the underlying Love that I am continues much the same. When the initial shock wears off, I ignore the people and their deeds. I still don't know about liking them, though."

"Should we just forget an event like the Oklahoma bombings and not take any action against the violators?" someone sitting behind me asked. Her voice was edged with impatience.

"Not at all," I replied. "I'm not asking any of you to like anybody or to ignore certain situations. When people commit such violent acts, they should be caught and dealt with. The public needs to be protected, and violence should end."

"So, you are human after all," Chrissie said, smirking. "I was beginning to wonder about you."

"That poor crab!" I thought. She poked at it again. "We should never forget that Love is who we *are*…or to allow anyone to cause us to become less than Loving towards all life."

"Oops!" Chrissie said, suddenly realizing how she was provoking a now very unhappy crab. "What are your views on hunting, fishing, shooting, and those sorts of things?" she asked.

"Well, I can't say I approve," I began. "But I can't see why you asked the question. Why do you think it's wrong to kill people but not animals?"

"That's heavy!" someone said. "People hunt and fish for fun, but they kill and hurt people out of malice. People are different …more sensitive."

"Somehow, I don't think the animal kingdom would appreciate the difference, do you?" I scoffed.

She didn't answer.

"You know," I said, trying to redirect the discussion, "I think we're missing the point of death in this talk."

"What's that?" Chrissie asked.

"…there's no such thing as death."

"Yes there is! I've been around too many graveyards to believe that we all wake up again on some judgment day." Chrissie was alert again and back into the discussion.

"No, Chrissie. You are wrong—well, not entirely. I have to agree that souls who have departed are not lying underground waiting to be called to account. But, you can't kill a spirit."

"Oh?"

"I'm talking about the spirit that lives in the body, the essential Love, which is you, your friends, and me."

"But, Malcolm, I don't feel different from my body. Aren't we one and the same?"

A ripple of laughter went through the group.

"Don't be flippant, Chrissie," I chided. "I've been trying for weeks to explain to you that the Love that you *are* is your spiritual awareness and that everything else is emotion, which gets in the way of reality, peace, happiness, and contentment. Move emotion to one side, especially fear and anger, and you begin to view life from a totally different place."

"You keep saying that…"

"Let me put it this way, Chrissie, I'm not in my body; I don't feel that I'm in my body. It's just something that I communicate through—a way of experiencing separateness. There is nothing in the world anyone can do to cause me to fear death."

"Wouldn't that depend on the way you die?"

"Then your fear is of the means, not of death."

"Oh…"

"Dying is not a problem for those who live in the awareness of Love; and I include birds, animals, and other life in this," I explained. "Even pain becomes less when fear is absent because pain is a symptom of fear.

"Is that really true?" Chrissie asked, sounding surprised.

"Oh, yes. You should be present when a healer is visiting the terminally ill. As spiritual Love enters the room, a wonderful peace descends on the scene; and one can almost see the fear disperse and the pain it causes to ease."

"Sounds truly beautiful," someone replied.

"It is. This is something that can't be logically explained. It's a profound experience—an experience of Love."

Quiet settled over the group as Chrissie and her friends considered their own fears, and lives. Speaking in a low voice, I said, "It's impossible to kill anything. All you can do is deprive the spirit of a physical experience."

"If that's true, Malcolm," someone asked, "why are you so against hunting, fishing, and shooting?"

"Because it is unnecessary and creates fear and loss. Love knows nothing of destruction—Love is creative."

"Creative?" Chrissie asked, sounding confused.

"To hurt another person, Chrissie, or to kill someone, you first have to destroy that part of the Love you are that would prevent you from killing."

"Explain that!"

"If a man goes out and shoots a bird, he first has to destroy something within himself, to be free to kill, and that something is

Love. Any form of hurt will spiritually cause more harm for the spirit of the offender than it ever will for the victim."

"This thought will make a lot of people feel worried when they hear it," someone in the group replied.

"Yes, I know, but it's a spiritual truth. Any person who does harm to another or to an animal must first destroy their own Love, to be free to cause harm. There are no exceptions to this law of Love."

"There are always exceptions," Chrissie said emphatically.

"No. You cannot say you did it for God. Anyone who does harm to another has first destroyed the Love in self that binds us to God. It's impossible to destroy another's Love. You might destroy their physical shell, but another's Love is beyond the reach of earthly humans. The greatest risk to our Love comes from ourselves."

"Just how far does this go?" asked a man in the group showing signs of concern.

"All the way," I replied. "If you want to say something hurtful, if you want to cause harm to another person without actually killing, you still have to destroy the Love in you to be free to hurt."

Chrissie wasn't ready to respond, so I added, "Love is your great protector, but you become vulnerable yourself to hurt if you remove your protective Love, in order to be free to hurt others."

"Can you get Love back? I mean, can you repair the damage?" Chrissie asked, speaking in a serious tone.

"First of all, Chrissie, those who have innocently suffered or hurt at the hands of another will be made whole again with God's great Love. But those who have chosen to destroy their own Love have to repair the damage themselves, which can be a long and painful experience."

"Are you sure, Malcolm?"

"It is a natural law, Chrissie. If you destroy your own Love to be free to hurt another, the wound you cause for yourself will pain you beyond imagination, once you return to spiritual awareness."

"Is it exactly the same if you shoot an animal, catch a fish, or hunt a fox?"

"Yes, Chrissie, it is the same. All life is valued equally in the spiritual realms."

"But what should I do if I notice a mouse in the kitchen?" Chrissie was being practical again.

"If you have a mouse in the kitchen, or you need to control wildlife for other reasons, it can be done without harming Love."

"That sounds very convenient."

"Let me finish."

"Sorry."

"It all goes back to the emotion or thought behind the killing. The Love element is unaffected if you are free from thoughts of pleasure, anger, or revenge...provided you are not killing to satisfy an emotion such as greed or superiority."

"Please, Malcolm, give us an example," someone said.

"Alright then, animals kill to eat; but they don't kill for fun, or pleasure, or to prove how great or clever they are. They don't kill to earn approval from God or humans. They just do it out of necessity."

"Have you ever killed for reasons other than necessity?" Chrissie asked, targeting her question for maximum impact. Everyone in the group was watching for my reaction. Her question was a fair one and needed answering.

"Yes, I have."

"How did you feel about it?" Her question was asked with love and sympathy, which I appreciated.

"Terrible the first time, but I soon got over it. Then, it became easy...easy because I had destroyed the Love in me, which earlier had prevented me from killing."

"What did you kill?"

Chrissie was poking the crab again, now using a stick she had picked up. She wasn't harming the crab. Rather, she was using it to help herself appear unconcerned about my answer; and she was feeling the difficulty I was having as I recalled an insensitive period of my life.

"Birds," I answered. "I was on a farm that was plagued by sparrows. They were getting into the buildings and soiling equipment and grain, as well as damaging growing crops during the summer."

"But surely that was Ok," Chrissie said protectively. "I mean that was to control."

"Your thought would make a nice excuse, Chrissie, but it wouldn't be true. I had an air rifle and was proud of the fact that I was quite a marksman. To me, it was sport—not control. I enjoyed it. Killing the sparrows made me no better than people who hunt and shoot big game, like deer. Size has nothing to do with it. Every life is precious. I have learned what it means to destroy my own Love."

"But, you're teaching others now."

"I was fortunate. I learned in time to start putting it right before full spiritual awareness was returned," I explained.

"How did you do that?" Chrissie was still feeling awkward about questioning me; but, somehow, she knew that it wasn't the crab in the rocks that she was prodding and agitating…it was me.

"I once had a dog that I loved, and watching him die in great pain was hurtful. No veterinarians were available when I needed one, so I had to end the dog's life myself. It was the most painful experience of my life, and my heart nearly broke. As I was preparing to release this suffering spirit of its torment, great calm came over me; and I heard the voice of Love say, 'Now you understand a little of the great sadness I suffer every time I have to release Love from suffering brought about by humans' selfish and unnecessary need to destroy the Love I gave life to.'"

"That's sad, Malcolm," Chrissie said.

"Sadness, not anger, is probably the best way to deal with destruction…sadness at what has been lost…sadness for the one who has caused the loss. Their hurt, when they eventually come to realize what they've done, will be excruciating; and eventually, even if it takes beyond this lifetime, they will come to know and feel the pain they caused others."

No one spoke a word. We all got up, in silent unison, and walked back to where the children were laughing and playing.

Chapter Seven
FORGIVENESS

"If you ask for forgiveness, will it always be granted?"

Chrissie was in one of her thoughtful moods. I was enjoying the quiet part of the week when she wandered in and sat down. I was busy writing and hadn't taken a lot of notice of her being there. She often came to sit in the spiritual quiet of our place of work.

"…would depend upon who you are asking, I suppose." My answer wasn't too serious—my thoughts were far away.

"I was thinking about what you told us last week…about how distressed you felt about those little birds you had to shoot," she said, trying to lead me into a discussion.

She had my attention now. "Are you asking if I prayed for forgiveness?"

"No, not really," Chrissie said thoughtfully, "but I was wondering if you would have felt better if you had prayed."

"Go on," I encouraged. Obviously, she had thoughts beneath those she had so far exposed.

"Well," she hesitated, "I'm still thinking of the people who kill children without any degree of regret. If they prayed and asked for forgiveness, would it be granted? It all seems too easy."

"Alright, Chrissie," I had now given up any thoughts of finishing my writing. "This question has several sides to it."

"Your answers usually do," she said, raising her eyes to look at me. I saw them smile.

"I don't suppose I do give a simple yes or no to anything, do I? If only life was that simple...but as I was saying, the question has several parts to it. Should we pray for forgiveness? Will God grant it if we do? Is the forgiveness, if granted, conditional in any way? Should victims of hurt be expected to grant forgiveness? Will victims of hurt benefit if they do forgive? Will victims suffer if they don't forgive?"

"Ay! Stop!," Chrissie said, trying to interrupt my flow of questions. "I don't like the last question, the one about whether victims will suffer if they don't forgive. Haven't they already suffered enough through no fault of their own? Should they also suffer the insult of being expected to say, 'It's ok. You killed my family, but I forgive you.'"

"Perhaps so, Chrissie, but aren't we told that forgiveness is good for the soul? I'm not saying I agree, but it is expected."

"You've done it again!" Chrissie said, gasping.

"Done what?"

"You've turned the whole argument upside down! We are now discussing the possible problems for the victims, if they don't forgive, instead of where I started, which was 'Can the abusers escape retribution by asking for forgiveness?'"

"Ok, Chrissie, I see your point; but we will have to come to that last question sooner or later. Let's begin by discussing the role of forgiveness and who is likely to use it or need it. Before the word can have any meaning at all, someone has to have been judged."

"What do you mean, Malcolm?"

"Well, you can't forgive someone until you have made a decision about whether they have done right or wrong."

"Right or wrong?"

"Give it some thought, Chrissie. In cases like murder, it's obviously a case of being wrong in every opinion, unless, of course, it's terrorists who have killed. Then, their bigoted ideology gives them an excuse for what they do, and they don't think they need forgiveness. People who are so devoid of spiritual values as to not value the Love of God in other people and who can't see wrong in destruction are outside of this discussion."

"Why?"

"Because, Chrissie, they have put themselves beyond spiritual help; but we can return to this question another time. The immediate danger is for those who have been hurt."

"You mean in a spiritual sense?" she asked.

"I mean in any sense. You see, Chrissie, if in their distress and grief, victims allow the anger they feel to become permanent, and if they *become* the anger, which will allow resentment to set in, it won't be long before they turn to hate."

"Oh, I understand what you're saying, Malcolm."

"Now, we have a real problem."

"Why?"

"Because hate demands satisfaction, release; and the only way it can do that, now that anger has replaced Love, is through vengeance, or revenge. The trouble with hate is that you become the anger when you change from Love; and the hate, or anger, continues—and so, has to be continually satisfied with revenge. Once isn't enough! Hate has an insatiable appetite for revenge, which keeps it alive."

"I can see where this is leading," Chrissie said thoughtfully. "It's very clear."

"The damage caused by the original evil or murder is now spreading fast. It has damaged, by death, emotional Love in at least a second person by setting up anger in the hearts of those who suffered the loss; and if that anger grows into hate and responds with violence to kill or hurt others, then the original act of violence is becoming guilty of creating a spiritual catastrophe."

"Phew!" gasped Chrissie. "…a sort of pyramid effect."

"An excellent simile…that's just what it is; and as long as the effect spreads, every layer in the pyramid will be responsible for the spiritual disintegrations of all of those in the layers beneath them."

"We're talking about a lot of people, now," Chrissie said, thinking aloud.

"Right. In terrorist campaigns that have gone on for centuries in the name of religion or some other ideology, those who started it are still suffering and bearing the consequences of the continued violence of today. In spiritual terms, that is hell."

"So, back to forgiveness…"

"Alright, Chrissie, what is the point of asking for forgiveness if you have created a chain reaction for hate, violence, or just plain anger? You can't ask for forgiveness until it's all over. Otherwise, it would be like asking for forgiveness before killing someone."

"Can the people who start family feuds, or a sequence of events causing violence lasting years, begin to grow spiritually before all of the consequences of their original actions are finished?"

"Definitely not, Chrissie, though they may change to become Love again and even start to want higher spiritual values."

"Why is that, Malcolm?"

"Because they are tied by a spiritual law to the consequences of their actions for as long as those actions continue, even if they've died and are now in the spiritual world. If they grew spiritually, their pain would grow as they become more spiritually aware of what they did. As spiritual Love, their agonies would become unbearable."

"What happens to them in the spiritual world?" Chrissie wanted to know.

"Remind me to tell you about that another time. Otherwise, you will accuse me of changing the subject again. We haven't finished with forgiveness yet."

"You're right. So, where were we?"

"Let's review. Anyone who sets into motion a chain of events causing or resulting in anger or violence is tied to the consequences of that anger or violence; and at some point in their spiritual awakening, they will have to make amends for the actions, for the total results of what they started, before they can begin working towards being one with God's Love."

"So, you are saying that asking for forgiveness will not allow you to get away without making some form of restitution," Chrissie said triumphantly.

"Yes, your understanding is correct."

"Then why didn't you say so right at the beginning and spare me from so much heavy thinking?"

"Because, Chrissie, we discussed only part of the answer."

"Oh no," she groaned. "I'm beginning to wish I hadn't started this."

"Well, I can stop, if you really want me to."

"No you can't!" she said, eyes twinkling. "Anyway, I'm ready for round two!"

"Brilliant! Let's get back to what God, Love, is likely to do if asked for forgiveness."

"Please do, Malcolm. I want to hear where He, Love, stands on the subject of forgiveness."

I couldn't restrain my smile. God was about to undergo a Chrissie-type interrogation. I hoped that someone had warned Him. "He wouldn't even recognize the request," I began.

"Why?" She was astonished by my statement.

"Because Love can only interact with Love, and Love is incapable of judgment. I have already explained that you can't forgive until you judge someone. Those people who forgive easily haven't even judged in the first place. Love accepts, totally, everybody as they are. It also recognizes that every spirit must move forward, from whatever situation it has created, by its own efforts—by making good the hurt it has caused."

"I'm getting confused again, Malcolm."

"In other words, forgiveness only has value when you are ready to forgive yourself by taking back to yourself all the hurt and suffering you have caused, to relieve others of it. It doesn't matter who grants forgiveness. Forgiveness is of no value to the people it is offered to until they begin to accept that they are not worthy of receiving it—until they can change to become Love."

"But what are the poor things suppose to do then?" a sympathetic Chrissie asked.

"You've switched sides, haven't you? A minute ago, you wanted the violators to suffer the full consequences of their actions; and now, you are feeling sorry for them."

"I know, but I want them to have some sense of being able to put it all right." Chrissie was being more forgiving now. "Do you know why you have become more forgiving towards offenders, Chrissie?"

"No, not really, but I can feel that I have," she said honestly.

"It's because the offenders have viewed themselves as you viewed them, unworthy of help. Can't you see, Chrissie, they have changed sides. They now view what they did as wrong, they want to put it right, and Love is always eager to help others' Love grow."

"I don't think…"

"Chrissie, everything changes the moment the offenders realize the hurt they have caused, or are causing, and want to put it right. Forgiveness is not even important to them now. They aren't interested in being forgiven, only in returning everything to the original state of Love."

"How can they do that?"

"…by spiritually experiencing all the hurt, pain, and fear they caused as a consequence of their actions. In other words, they can dissolve the emotions of anger, hate, etc., which they originally brought into being, by becoming Love. Usually, some great personal catastrophe is required—one that breaks the personality, breaks into the self-centered emotions—to cause the change and the wave of sorrow that sweeps over the ones who have been lost to hate, jealously, and other emotions. In that moment, Love has an opportunity to break free and to see what damage has been done."

"What if the pyramid is still growing?" I detected a note of anxiety in Chrissie's voice.

"Then spiritually, offenders must do something to stop it, or their pain will grow."

"But, Malcolm, if they've died and are in the spirit world, how can they do that?"

Chrissie was now putting all of her loving concern into finding ways to help the offenders in my examples to find a way back to a state of Love. "That's where reincarnation comes in. Rebirth gives them an opportunity to come back and change what they started."

"On their own?" Chrissie asked. "Isn't anyone going to help them?"

I smiled and said, "Well I'm sure they've already got one supporter in you."

She smiled back. "So, Malcolm, what does that mean?"

"It means you've forgiven them…accepted them as they are, without judgment. When fallen Love recognizes what it has done and starts trying to put everything right without blaming others or looking for excuses, it has begun the long, painful journey back to its proper spiritual self; and all around, there will be Love, like yours, ready and willing to offer encouragement and hope."

"I didn't really say that I had forgiven…"

"Forgiveness only comes when it isn't asked for. That's because the offenders have judged themselves unworthy of it in their present state and want to do something about it, by changing the emotions that caused them to lose their Love in the beginning. It's hard, Chrissie, very hard to have to admit you were wrong and to accept responsibility for the pain and suffering you caused by your actions of some earlier time."

"How did you do that?"

"Do what?"

"You know, Malcolm. I started off angry and unforgiving and finished up feeling sorry for offenders and trying to help them."

"I think you changed when you realized that God, as Love, wasn't going to do anything. Loves doesn't do anything. It just is. If God had stepped in to put everything right, you wouldn't have done anything; and you might still be angry."

"Yes, you're right."

"God knows the depth of your Love, Chrissie, and the Love of others. So, He waits for you to stop judging and to begin accepting. In that way, the Love you are will cause the change."

"So…"

"Remember, Chrissie, it's not what you do or say, whether you forgive or don't forgive, that will cause a change. It is who you *are* that causes changes from abuse to Love. It's the Love that radiates from you that is so powerful."

Chrissie went silent; I returned to my writing.

Chapter Eight
LOVE OR BURDEN

"Chrissie phoned; she wants to see you," Debbie said, as I arrived for the day.

"What did you tell her?"

"...that you had an available appointment this afternoon between four and five."

"Does she have a problem? Or just want to chat?"

"She wants to talk to you about a friend who is terminally ill, I think," Debbie replied, turning her attention from me to the phone, which was being particularly vocal that morning.

My first client of the day came in and sat down. I guessed that she was about seventy; and from the moment she entered, I could sense her attitude of calm and inner contentment. She exuded the sort of confidence that comes with years of dealing with life's problems in a quiet, uncomplaining way. She was the sort of lady everybody should have as a grandmother, a harbor of calm in the rough ocean of life. I guessed she had given many hours of comfort and love to family and friends in their hours of need.

One of the wonderful things about being a healer is that one gets to see so many beautiful people. Most of the people who come asking for help are truly loving people. When I get to know them, I learn that most of them have given of themselves to help others. With some, it's just giving time and love to the lonely and aged in the area. Such love is never measured. It just is. I distinctly remember one lady of over ninety who apologized for being late for an appointment. "I've been doing the shopping for some old people who find it difficult to get around," she said, apologetically.

"How old are they?" I asked. If she was ninety, I thought that the neighborhood she lived in must have found the elixir of life.

"In their seventies and eighties, poor dears. They have difficulty getting about, you know, because of their years."

"How can I possibly help you?" I asked, smiling. "You are fitter and probably more healthy than I am."

"Oh, I don't think so," she replied. "I could pop off at any time. It will be nice to be gone from life's little difficulties, but I worry about who is going to care for my old ladies when I'm gone."

I have many angels visit my office, and I sensed that another of God's angels was with me that day. It's as if God says to these beautiful souls, "As much as you do for me, so I will now do for you. Go and see a spiritual healer."

I have no doubt, and have never had any doubts, that most of the people who come for help are spiritually guided my way because of the love and help they have given to others during their lives; and this lady was no exception. My time with her was lovely and got my day off to a beautiful start.

Chrissie usually had some burning question, which wouldn't wait another minute; but today, she was quiet and reflective. As she seemed reluctant to begin the conversation, I said something about what a inspirational morning I'd had and what a beautiful day it was.

"How would you know?" she asked, but not expecting a reply. "You spend all day in here—you never see the daytime sun."

"I was thinking more about the people I've seen, than the weather. It's a beautiful day because of them."

"What sort of problems did they have?" she asked.

"The people I've seen today don't think they have any

problems...just wanted me to help ease their pain a little. One wanted to know how to help her mother who is terminally ill; another is terminally ill, herself, and was worried about being a burden on her family, rather than focused on herself."

"Don't you find that a big responsibility, Malcolm?" Chrissie had begun to come from within herself.

"Yes, I suppose." She was obviously using that thought to help her with some difficulties of her own.

"How do you try to convince someone who's dying that they're not a burden on their family?"

We were now beginning to get to the point of her visit. "Who have you in mind?"

"My grandmother." Chrissie's eyes were watery, and she reached across for a tissue.

"You are going to need another box of these after I'm gone," she said, trying to smile and appear lighthearted.

In the presence of Love, sorrow will always surface. It is only a reflection of Love and nothing to be ashamed of. I waited. Chrissie would continue when she was ready.

"I have the greatest Grandmom in the world," she started, "and it's breaking my heart to watch her get weaker."

I already knew that Chrissie's grandmother had become weak and frail very quickly over the past months. She had always been a very independent lady, in a loving way, and had continued to live and manage on her own, even after her husband died about twelve years earlier.

"Is she still on her own?"

"That's one of the problems, Malcolm. She should move in with my parents, or at least move to a place where she will have constant love and care."

"Why doesn't she?"

"Gandmom won't go to my parents because they live so far away; and, anyway, she doesn't want to leave her home."

"What about you?"

"She could come to me, of course, but I live in a tiny upstairs apartment, which isn't practical. And, she lives too far from where I work for me to move in with her."

"Does anyone call around to see her?"

"Oh yes, she has plenty of friends, but they're all a bit like Grandmom, old and unsteady. I visit her several times a week and most weekends, but it's distressing to see her like she is now. She used to be very active, but now spends more and more time in bed."

"Is she in pain?"

"She wouldn't let me know if she is," Chrissie's voice became exasperated.

"That's one of the problems, Malcolm. She never complains …never asks for help. She just tells me not to worry about her. Grandmom doesn't want to be a burden to anyone. So, of course, I worry even more."

"How do you think I can help?"

"I don't think you can help. She would be furious if she knew I told you."

"Right."

"Actually, Malcolm, I was wondering…could you tell me how to help her?"

"You seem to be doing all you can Chrissie, giving her lots of love and attention."

"But that's the whole problem," Chrissie began to explain. "It's as if she's resisting my love. She gets upset when I buy her little things—says I should save my money. When I phone to see how she is, she makes excuses to put the phone down, saying that she doesn't want to run up my phone bill. I know I shouldn't let her comments bother me, but they hurt. I know she does these things only because she loves me and doesn't want to be a bother, but she doesn't seem to realize that I enjoy looking after her. I want to do things for her."

I said nothing.

"She was wonderful to me when I was little and was always

there when I had problems. Grandmom was able to help without being critical of me. She was there when I needed someone to talk to; and now, when she needs my help, she won't let me."

Chrissie was now deep into the box of tissues. "Have you told her how you feel?"

"I've tried, but she just smiles and says, 'Don't worry about me, Chrissie. You have your whole life ahead of you.' Sometimes, she sounds as if she doesn't expect to be here much longer."

Chrissie tugged at another handful of tissues. "Why are old people so difficult?" she asked with a tone of impatience.

I couldn't help smiling. "I think it's a case of Grandmother's patience being stronger than yours."

"What's that suppose to mean?" she demanded.

"Chrissie," I began slowly, thinking how best to help them both. "Chrissie, your Grandmother is not unlike millions of other grandmothers all over the world. They have spent their whole lives caring for and looking after other family members. They probably started by looking after their own grandmothers! When Grandmother was a little girl and part of a large household, she probably didn't get a lot of love and attention. With so many to look after, Grandmother, as a little girl, was probably ignored—not unkindly, but just because of the demands of the adults. Remember, there were no washing machines, freezers, vacuum cleaners, and all of the other luxuries of life that we take for granted today. So everyone was busy caring for someone else. Your Grandmother probably grew up caring for others but not learning how to be cared for."

"You mean Grandmom is embarrassed by my wanting to do things for her?"

Chrissie was incredulous. "That's exactly what I mean—she feels awkward when you buy little things. It wasn't something she grew up to expect."

"But that's not true," Chrissie said. "She's received presents, like the rest of the family."

"Yes, I know...but as often as she gets them now? Most

weeks you give her some little thing as a token of your love, and she isn't used to this kind of giving. She doesn't know how to deal with it."

"But, can't she just accept that I want to give her gifts and do things for her? Can't she just accept them to make me happy?"

"Chrissie, your Grandmother is a lovely, old lady; and you want to change her ways to suit yourself."

She didn't answer.

"At eighty-eight, I don't think she has to do anything she doesn't want to do, do you? If you can understand what I'm saying, then you won't feel hurt. You are expecting Grandmother to change roles with you."

"Please, Malcolm, explain what you mean." Chrissie was softer now.

"All her life, Grandmother has been the giver, the provider, and the comforter; and now, when she is least able to change her ways, you are asking her to be the taker, to be comforted. Chrissie, she doesn't know how to be the way you want her to be."

"I hadn't thought of it like that."

I enjoyed a moment of silence as Chrissie thought about my comments.

"What am I supposed to do then, nothing?" she asked, sounding petulant.

"Come on, Chrissie, snap out of it. She wants your love and understanding more now than ever before. Do what you've always done. Tell her what you are doing—ask her advice about this or that. Ask her to do little things for you. Instead of buying her things, make things just for her, bake a cake or paint a picture for her. Now is the time for you to be aware of her needs by being sensitive to her fears and uncertainties."

"Oh Malcolm, this is so frustrating! How can I be aware of her needs? If I ask, she always says that she doesn't need or want anything."

"Of course she will. You must be the wise one. Notice what

she wants and get it anyway without making a fuss. A sort of unwritten conversation will pass between you. This would have been easier for your mother because she and Grandmother would have had a closer dialogue."

"So do it without causing embarrassment?"

"You know, Chrissie, a lot of people, as they get older, worry about being a burden on their family. All their lives, they have had the joy of caring for and helping others. It's because they have had the opportunity to care for others that their own Love has grown."

"Grandmom is full of Love."

"If no one on Earth needed help, if everyone was healthy and fit, and if everybody had all they wanted, Love would have no way of experiencing the need to give of itself. Love would have no way to grow. This way, we spend most of our lives caring for others so that our Love can grow."

"Then we get older," Chrissie thought aloud.

"Right. In the last few years of our lives, as if to say 'thank you' for all the opportunities we've had to let our Love grow, we become dependent upon others, family and friends, to give them the opportunity to let their Love develop."

"Love or burden?" Chrissie muttered under her breath.

"…Love, Chrissie." Near the end of my life, I won't mind if I need to be cared for or helped in some way. If so, it'll be a way of saying 'thank you' for all of the wonderful happiness I've experienced while helping others."

"I agree," said Chrissie, who had pushed away the tissue box. "I love looking after my Grandmom, and I can see what you mean about her being embarrassed."

"Why not tell her what we've just discussed. She probably hasn't thought about things this way. Or, Chrissie, have you thought of asking Grandmother to do something for you…something like rooting a cutting from her favorite houseplant, just something to help her feel useful and appreciated?"

"Those are good ideas, Malcolm. Do you think I'll be like

Grandmom one day?"

"I don't know, Chrissie. Many of today's young people have never had to care about anyone but themselves, which is totally the opposite of Grandmother's generation; so they'll probably expect to have everything done for them."

"You make me sound very selfish."

"I didn't mean to, Chrissie. Life today is just different than it was when Grandmother was a youngster. A lot of young people don't even begin to work until they are in their late teens or early twenties; and because of all of the modern household appliances, they have no need to help around the house much or to work and help with the family income."

"You sound as if you don't approve of labor-saving devices," Chrissie groaned.

"Yes I do! I wouldn't want to have to do the sort of work my grandparents did."

"People sure use their time differently nowadays."

"Have you noticed how many younger people are looking for ways to be helpful to their communities?" I asked.

"Without the old close family system, when all the family lived together, people will continue to find other ways to express their Love, particularly through community works," Chrissie agreed.

"People are looking to experience awareness, Chrissie. That's one of the reasons you come to listen to what I have to say. No doubt, you also read lots of books on spiritual matters."

"You're right," she replied. "I find myself reading more and more about life's energies, meditation, and things like that. Does meditation help?"

"Oh yes. People who meditate are always easier to help. I always know if someone meditates—they go farther into the higher energy fields or spiritual realms." "There you go again, Malcolm, passing comments about these spiritual fields, but you haven't told me anything about them yet. By the way, you still haven't kept your promise about explaining what you know about reincarnation."

she said, getting up to leave.

"But you never remind me until you're about to leave."

"Can I come sometime next week?"

"You had better ask Debbie, but I expect Love will have a place for you somewhere in the appointment book."

Chapter Nine
DEATH AND DYING

"It's me again."

"Thanks, Chrissie, where's yours?" A look of disbelief crossed her face as I relieved her of her soda.

"Oh, sorry," she said, grinning. "I didn't know you wanted one."

"What's the topic to be this time?"

"I've been wondering what it must be like when a person dies." She gave me a funny look.

"That's a bit gruesome…today's a lovely bright day; and as far as I can tell, you are perfectly fit and healthy. Why would someone with everything to live for want to think about death?"

"I didn't say I had been thinking about death," she answered rather coldly. "I've been thinking about how it must be to die—to go from here to there. You have already taught me enough to know there is no death, just transition. So I assume you must know something about the experience."

"Sorry," I said, "but most people are unable to separate the difference between death and transition."

"How would you differentiate between the two, Malcolm?"

"I would say that death is when it happens to someone else. To those who remain, the one who has gone has died. It all seems very final. The body is buried or cremated, and nothing remains except the memories. Spiritually aware people will have a different perception; but to the rest, it is over, final. It's death of a body."

"Of a body?"

"Yes, Chrissie. To the one who has left the body, death is just a transition from one state of awareness to another…a process of change to be reborn in another place. To those who have gone, it's not about memories at all—but about the future."

"Is the other side always a future to look forward to?" she asked, looking concerned.

"What awaits us on the other side is a big subject; and before we get onto that topic, let's talk about how we get there."

"Have you been with people when they died?"

"Yes, Chrissie, often."

"What's it like?"

"…depends on the situation. Dying can be a most beautiful and spiritual experience or it can be distressing. I've witnessed both."

"But why should one be beautiful and one scary?"

"…fear, Chrissie. Most people have the wrong perception about death or dying; and they've been taught that something less than beautiful awaits them if they have any guilt in their lives. This, of course, is nonsense."

"Please explain."

"Sometimes, the actual process of dying takes place over months, as the Love or spiritual energy begins to disentangle itself from the physical and emotional energies it has been working with. Those who are full of Love will find the act of slowly, or even quickly, becoming separate from their physical and emotional selves quite easy. First, they start to become more intuitive, more perceptive."

"Why more perceptive?"

"As the spirit becomes less a part of the physical, it will perceive spiritual activity it would not normally notice."

"What sort of spiritual activity?" Chrissie was leaning forward and listening carefully.

"...being aware of a spiritual presence in the room with them."

"How does a person do that?"

"By becoming sensitive to vibrations they wouldn't normally notice."

"Sounds very complicated," Chrissie said.

"Really, it isn't. Lots of people, knowingly or unknowingly, pick up other people's emotions—especially if a Love bond exists between them. Pain is a good example."

"You mean some people, who are spiritually perceptive, can actually feel another's pain?"

"Don't look so shocked, Chrissie. I've known lots of people who've taken pain-killing drugs or had medical examinations for problems that weren't theirs."

"You're kidding. Like who? Can you give me an example?" she was fascinated.

"We are going off of the subject a little, but alright. I remember a lady who asked for healing but gave no reason. I obliged; and within a few minutes, I was experiencing a very severe pain in the area of my liver."

"What did you do, Malcolm?"

"I looked at the lady and asked: 'You think you have cancer of the liver, don't you?'"

"What did the lady say?"

"She sat quietly for a few seconds. Then she asked, 'How did you know?'"

"I was just about to ask the same question, Malcolm."

I ignored Chrissie's remark and continued. I replied: "I have a severe pain in the area of my liver, and I know it's not my pain because it started when you arrived. So the pain must be coming from you. Your thoughts read out as cancer, and I just understand that you think you have cancer."

"Go on," Chrissie said.

"The lady looked at me and said, 'Do I?'"

"Well…did she?"

"Oh, be quiet, Chrissie, and let me finish."

"Sorry."

"No, she didn't have cancer, and I was able to explain that the pain wasn't hers."

"How could you possibly know?" Chrissie beat me this time.

"That's exactly what the lady asked."

"Sorry, Malcolm."

"I explained that what I was feeling was an emotional energy not a physical energy; so I interpreted that to mean that the pain was coming through her and not from her."

"But how did you know that?" Chrissie was on the edge of her seat.

"Come on, Chrissie, this was only a normal healing session. It's my job to know."

"So tell me," she said. "Or is it some great secret? If so, I'll sign on as the sorcerer's apprentice; and then, you can tell me."

"Cut the clowning long enough, and I'll tell you," I replied. "Anyway, what do you mean…sorcerer's apprentice?"

She laughed.

"Physical energy has a warmth about it. When I put my hand over someone and feel a warmth, I know I'm experiencing their physical vibrations. If, however, I put my hands over someone and feel coolness in their vibrations, then I know I'm dealing with emotional energy or problems."

"You do this with every client?"

"No, I don't always have to hold my hands over people to know if their vibrations are warm or cold. Once you become spiritually perceptive, you can do it from any distance."

"But if the pain wasn't the lady's, whose was it?" Chrissie asked, acting as if we were about to solve some big mystery.

"I asked her who in the family might have a liver problem. She told me that her husband was an alcoholic. So there was the answer to the lady's pain. Her husband was drinking too much, damaging his liver. His wife, out of love and concern, was picking up the vibrated energy of his liver disintegration. She was actually experiencing his pain."

"Fascinating, Malcolm."

"She also told me that she was scheduled for medical tests. I had no hesitation in telling her the tests would be clear, which she later confirmed."

"Would she have to go on suffering her husband's pain?"

Chrissie asked the same question that lots of people ask when they realize their pain or discomfort is from someone else. "No. Once a person determines that the pain isn't theirs, they can ignore it."

"Ignore it? How does a person do that?"

"Once we logically realize that the pain we are experiencing isn't our own, the subconscious, which is picking it up, ignores the vibrations. A bit like only tuning into the voices you want to hear in a crowded room and ignoring the others."

I paused to collect my thoughts. "Now where are we?"

"…the dying becoming more spiritually aware."

"Oh, yes. As we start to disentangle from our own physical body, we become more aware of the energy vibrations of others. This process continues until, eventually, we also begin to disentangle from our emotional energy."

"But if we leave our emotions behind, we have no sense of anything, right?" Chrissie said, butting in.

"Yes, we do. Don't forget, we are Love; emotion is something separate. It's what we do, think, or say. Love is who we *are*, remember?"

"But, Malcolm, what if we have anger, as you explained a few weeks ago. Remember? You said that instead of experiencing the anger, we become so much part of it that the Love element is diminished."

"Yes, Chrissie, I remember. If we've become the anger, then that begins to show through more clearly. Whatever emotion we've become in place of the Love will begin to exhibit itself more clearly the closer we come to our transition."

"Does that mean that it's not only Love or anger that we can become?"

"That's right. Fear is the biggest obstacle to a peaceful transition from life in human form to life in spiritual form. If people, once they realize that they are passing over, would relax and let the normal process work, they would have no difficulties. Dying would be a beautiful experience. Instead, they fight to stay awake and in control; and they suffer the agonies of a dying body that is trying to release them."

"Fear…a real obstacle," Chrissie said, thinking aloud and making a mental note.

"The fear I just mentioned is, of course, different from the fear experienced involving some other situation," I added.

"Right."

"The fear of dying leaves us once the transition is made, but fear caused by the circumstances immediately before death gets trapped in our emotional energy and remains a part of our emotional energy when we are reborn."

"Are you describing my experience?" Chrissie asked.

"That's right. Your spirit became fear and pain at the time of death, and so it remained in your psyche or your emotional field. When you were reborn, the only way you could release the fear was to let you experience it again, or to recall it in some way."

"Why?"

"Because if you can bring it to logical awareness, you can satisfy the demands of the pain or fear. Once you are aware of what's causing the inner anxiety or the pain, you can deal with the problem logically."

"I see."

"It's much more difficult if hate, jealousy, envy, or other such emotions are involved, though. They take a lot of working through before Love can conquer."

"So what you're saying, Malcolm, is that whatever emotion you die with, you will bring it back with you when you're reborn."

"You're absolutely right, Chrissie. Moving from this world to the next should be a peaceful experience, one that people can look forward to—not an experience of fear due to social ignorance."

"Wow, Malcolm, we all have a great responsibility to remove fear from people's lives, especially in places like hospitals. I think we need some education in this area."

"Brilliant, Chrissie. Everyone should know that the emotions they have become, Love, anger, jealousy, etc., are what they take with them to the other side, to the spiritual dimension. It's what they've become that decides what state or dimension they go to."

"Oh, I see. People could take any emotion with them."

"Right, the emotion you experience as a passing emotion can involve anything, possibly work-related needs, addictions, quick tempers, contentedness, joy, fears of illness—anything that is an underlying emotion controlled by the subconscious. Whatever, this emotion will wait around until you are reborn to reattach itself to you."

"I don't understand how emotions can just 'wait around,' as you put it, as if they were some independent being," Chrissie said, looking puzzled. "Surely they disperse into the atmosphere or something, and how do they find you again when you are ready to be reborn? Do these emotions affect anyone else while waiting for you?"

I was about to answer Chrissie's questions when she jumped in with another.

"Oh yes, and how big is this collection of emotions?"

"You are going to have to change your ways of thinking, Chrissie. We are now operating at another level of vibrational activity."

"This discussion is getting a bit beyond me," Chrissie said, sitting back in her chair and thinking for a moment.

"It's all quite easy, really. Once you have withdrawn to the spiritual world, the emotions you leave behind are held together by the attraction of their own vibrational activity. They can't disperse—there's nothing to cause them to disperse."

"Can you describe the emotional body for me, Malcolm? This part is a bit vague for me."

"I suppose that the best way to describe the emotional body is to say that it's as a fog, which remains once the physical activity of the body has released you. This 'fog' has your thought vibrations in it; so when you are born, it is immediately attracted back to you.'

"Does this happen before birth?" Chrissie asked.

"Yes, it does. An unborn child has a whole set of emotions waiting for it, which influence the baby at any time from three to four months after conception."

"Is that why children within a family can be so different?"

"Absolutely, but you are getting off the subject, Chrissie. We can discuss birth another time—let's stay with dying at the moment."

"Ok, but it's all so interesting."

Chrissie wanted to have the jig-saw I was building completed after the first two pieces had come together. "The trouble is, Chrissie, in trying to put this sort of explanation together, you can't see the complete picture until all of the pieces are in place."

"Tell me what you mean, Malcolm."

"Let's get back to emotion. Once the spirit has departed from the body, the emotion it leaves behind can be so strong that others can feel it…can be affected by it."

"Would that be like going into a house and feeling the atmosphere? Once, I decided not to move into an apartment because it didn't feel happy. Do you know what I mean? The apartment had a sad feeling about it."

"Very good, Chrissie. That's it. The emotion of a departed spirit can be so strong that it can be seen at times, when the energy forces holding it together take the shape of the form it used to be. In certain circumstances, emotional bodies are illuminated."

"Wow!" said Chrissie. "Ghosts."

"Yes, oftentimes, we think that we see or sense spirit people after someone dies; but actually, we're perceiving their emotions. That's why people often report a 'cold' sensation in the area where ghosts are supposed to be. Cold is associated with emotion."

"Why?"

"Let's stay with the subject, Chrissie."

"Oh, alright. What have I forgotten?" she asked, smiling.

"Today's topic is death and dying; and we've gotten a bit off track, haven't we? It's about the strength of physical energy to hold us to the body and the energy of emotion to affect the attitudes we have during the last months, weeks, or hours before we die. We may have brought the emotion into being; but as we come to have less control over the mind, so the emotions we created begin to control us. Fear is the biggest factor affecting a peaceful transition."

"So, are you saying," she went on, "that the emotions I create in my life won't disperse when I die? Will they sit around waiting for me until I come back?"

"Yes, that's right."

"How do you know this, Malcolm?"

"Because I am spirit living independently of the body, I can see beyond my physical eyes."

"You can see emotion?" she asked.

"Of course, Chrissie, it's like looking at an aura."

"I wondered when that word would come up," she said with a rather harsh tone.

"What don't you like about the word?" I asked.

"Well, it's the *in* word. People who claim to be spiritual generally say they can see auras. I sometimes think it's like Hans Christian Anderson's story of the king's clothes. You must know the story," she said. "It's about two tailors who con a king into thinking they've sold him a magnificent suit of clothes that are so pure only intelligent people can see them. The king, not wanting to admit to being slow-witted says he can see the suit, when of course there's nothing there; and so he goes out dressed only in his birthday suit."

"And how does the story relate to auras, Chrissie?"

"I've looked and looked for auras," she went on, "but I've never seen one. Then someone says, 'Look at that aura!' and I feel goofy because I can't see it. I've been tempted to say, 'Oh yes, isn't it pretty!' …to be like the king."

"Seeing auras is just a matter of altering your focus, really," I replied. "Most people look at what is solid and not at the space around the solid object, or person."

"How do you do that?"

Chrissie was interested and very much wanted to see an aura in spite of doubting their existence. "Most people look at objects. The next time you try to see an aura, look at the space around the person instead of looking directly at the person. You'll see the aura easier if the person is standing in front of a darker color such as dark blue or crimson. Lighter shades make it more difficult. Eventually, you will see a sort of heat haze around people, which is the energy field. With practice, you will soon begin to see it in color."

Just then, I realized that we were off the subject again. "But look, Chrissie, we are getting a long way from our subject of leaving the body."

"Yes, I suppose we are." She looked at the clock and seemed to realize that I wouldn't finish the discussion of death and dying if we didn't stop side-tracking. "Alright," she said, "But I'm keeping a note of my questions for other times. I promise not to interrupt again."

"A good act if you can do it, Chrissie," I said, laughing.

She returned a smile, and I returned to the subject matter. "Now, where have we gotten to? Oh, I remember. Someone is due to pass from this world to the next…it's a preordained thing, except, of course, for accidents and the like; but, as I said, in most cases the day and the way we leave is a very organized affair, if we allow it to be."

"So, for most people, death doesn't occur in just a moment?" Chrissie said, making another mental note.

"Right. A person who is spiritually preparing to pass over first begins the process of disentanglement from the physical body, and then the emotional body. As the process continues, the physical body becomes less able to contain the spirit."

I could see from Chrissie's face that she was struggling with her temptation to interrupt, so I answered her unspoken question. "The physical body has energy running through it," I said, "and this energy causes an electromagnetic field to build up around the body. This electronic field acts as a sort of electronic lock and prevents us from leaving the body. As the body's energies weaken, so the electromagnetic field loses its strength to keep us in the body, and we start to drift out."

"Thank you, Malcolm. I'm trying to be very good and not interrupt."

I continued. "If their energy levels fall below a certain level, a person can have an out-of-body experience. Often, this happens during a surgical operation when the patient drifts out of the body and watches the operation from a distance. Or it might happen when a person is very stressed or low on energy—they might leave the body and then see it from another part of the room."

"…so strange."

"Lots of people have out-of-body experiences, Chrissie. There's nothing very strange about it. Most people don't like discussing their experiences because of fear of being laughed at."

"What if a person gets stuck outside their body?"

"Unless we're dying, the energy levels can easily be raised to attract us back to the body."

"Yes, back to dying," Chrissie said, prompting herself.

"Right, back to the dying process. Once we leave the body at the physical level, we begin the final part of the transition by moving from the emotional body. People who have experienced near-death situations describe this as floating or rushing through a tunnel and moving towards the light. The tunnel is their own emotional field, which they are separating from."

"But why travel through the center of the tunnel?" Chrissie said, forgetting her promise.

"Because we don't move away from emotional energy in the same way we move from physical energy. It's more like an instant and concentrated meditation procedure."

"Meditation? I don't get it," Chrissie muttered.

"Try this way, Chrissie. If you practice meditation, you know how to concentrate on a single thought. Right? You practice stilling the mind until all thinking processes come to a halt. In that instant you have moved into the center of emotional awareness; you're at the center of your emotional attitudes, where you feel peace and contentment because the emotion is not part of you any more—it's around you."

"Got it, so far, Malcolm."

"At the moment of dying, your body lacks the physical energy to hold you; and so the attractive forces of the spiritual suck you up through your emotional field, and into the light, or spiritual world."

"So as you can see," I said, feeling rather pleased with myself at having put a difficult explanation across rather simply, "dying is quite easy and nothing to be afraid of. It's just an extended, instant form of meditation."

"How can you possibly say it's easy?" Chrissie came straight back at me.

I looked at the clock and hoped our time was nearly up. Chrissie with a problem to solve was a bit like a dog with a bone. She wouldn't give up until she had chewed every last smell out of it, and I felt a bit like a bone being chewed on. "Go on," I volunteered, "we've got a few more minutes."

"My friend's mother was dying of cancer, and the doctors expected her to last just a few more hours. So, my friend, Joan, promised to stay with her mother until she passed over—Joan promised her mother to be there when she died."

"Lots of people make such promises. Go on, Chrissie."

"Three days later, and although Joan's mother was still

suffering, she wasn't showing signs of becoming physically weaker. So, apart from leaving for a few minutes to go to the bathroom, Joan didn't leave her mother for three days."

Chrissie was in full flight now, and I knew from experience that it was best to wait until she had exhausted the explanation.

"At the end of the third day, Joan went home to do something for her husband. The doctors and nurses said that her mother hadn't changed in three days, and they didn't think she would alter much during the next two hours. Joan was gone for three hours; and when she returned, her mother had died. For three days, not three hours as the doctors originally expected, the poor lady struggled with dying."

I looked at the clock as Chrissie continued. "She eventually died alone."

The next few seconds seemed like hours as I wanted for Chrissie's ending.

"So..." she finally said, giving me a look that suggested she was daring me to argue. "How can you possibly say dying is easy?"

"Chrissie, please, just think for a minute. Didn't I say that a person can't leave their body unless the energy levels are low enough?"

"Yes, and obviously hers weren't."

"Exactly, Chrissie, and where do you think Joan's mother was getting the energy to sustain her life?"

"I don't know, Malcolm. She must have been stronger than the medical people thought."

"No, Chrissie, Joan was the one who was keeping her mother alive. The love bond between them made it possible for Joan to pass her energy into her mother's body, especially if she held her mother's hand. So the mother couldn't die, simply because Joan was energizing her body."

Chrissie's jaw dropped so far I thought I would have to pick it off the floor. "That's why the mother died while Joan was away. She couldn't die while Joan was there, can't you see?"

"And Joan has been feeling guilty for months because she thought she'd broken a promise. Surely, Malcolm, you're not saying we should leave people to die on their own?"

"No, of course not; and once you realize the mechanics of energy transference, you can control your own energy flow."

"How?"

"It's not something you do consciously, but once you know how at a subconscious level, you tend to withhold energy."

Debbie knocked on the door and came in.

"Excuse me, Malcolm, the next clients are here."

"Thanks, Debbie. Chrissie will come out with you."

"I will!" Chrissie said, giving me a big smile.

"I've already got my question for next week, Malcolm."

"Yes, I thought you might…"

Chapter Ten
A SPIRITUAL WORLD

"Hey Malcolm, can I tape these conversations?" Chrissie asked.

"…if you want to; but I think it better if you don't."

"How come?" she pressed.

"Because, Chrissie, if you're not careful, you only listen to other people's beliefs and experiences and become so engrossed in the tapes that you stop thinking and developing your own awareness."

"But where can I get answers like the ones you give, especially if I can't remember all you've said?"

"If you listen to your questions in your own mind, the answers come to you. I'm asking you to move into a higher level of energy or dimension where all of the information you want is available."

"Can you teach me how to do that, Malcolm?"

"If you'd like."

"I don't know what to do first," she admitted. "I've got a great question for today, but I also want to learn how to get into those higher thoughts."

"What's the question? Maybe I can answer it and help move you into higher thoughts at the same time."

Chrissie took a piece of paper out of her pocket and looked at what she had written before coming to my office. I could see she wasn't going to ask the question she had prepared and was reforming another question in her mind. "You want to know if people's awareness alters when they pass over, don't you?" I asked, laughing.

"You can't read my note from over there, can you?"

"Of course I can't, Chrissie. I just read your thoughts, and I think I can answer your question and teach you how to search the higher dimensions for answers—at the same time."

"I'm ready!" she said.

"Do you know how to meditate? Can you calm yourself and still your mind?"

Chrissie said that she did. Like most other people who have tried to meditate only a few times, however, she had great difficulty bringing her thoughts to a standstill. "Every time I sit quietly and try to focus on a single thought, my mind wanders to other subjects, she admitted."

"Of course it will, Chrissie. The subconscious doesn't want you to go back into the center of your emotions because it thinks that you might be off into the light…that it will lose control. What do you see when you're concentrating, or rather meditating, which is really the opposite of concentrating?"

"Whatever I'm focusing on," she said thoughtfully, "but isn't that concentrating?"

"It is to start with; but eventually, when your thoughts come under your command, you will be able to relax on a single thought. Again, when you meditate, what do you see, Chrissie? I mean…let's say you concentrate on a prayer. What exactly do you see?"

"Well, I don't see anything, I suppose. I just remain focused on the words of the prayer for as long as I can."

"In other words, you simply empty your mind of pictures?" I prompted.

"I hadn't thought about it; but, yes, I suppose I do."

"Right, Chrissie, and because you don't have a picture, you don't have anything to be emotional about. You are just repeating the words of a prayer."

"Yes, I usually meditate on a prayer or a verse."

"Any prayer or words will do, Chrissie, so long as they don't conjure up a picture for your mind to build on."

"Where's all of this leading, Malcolm?"

"I want you to move beyond meditation, Chrissie. You see, in order to interrelate with life, you need to have a picture in your mind. Animals don't have a vocabulary; however, they have a picture library—they 'think pictures' to each other."

"So…"

"If I want to commune with animals, I tune in to their thought vibrations and think in pictures. You'd be wasting your time if you thought or said 'It's cold tonight' and expected your pet to understand."

"I'm with you, Malcolm."

"However, if you created a scene in your mind of a frosty-looking garden, your pet, provided you are tuned in to the same vibrations, would pick up your pictures and know what's going through your thoughts."

"Can animals really do that?" Chrissie asked, expressing her surprise.

"Of course they can. Do you think that animals don't communicate, just because they don't use words? The picture library of the animal world is usually based on symbolism; and once you are able to tune in and use the same symbols as pictures in your mind, animals will respond."

"Really?"

"Believe me, Chrissie, the picture library is a far more efficient and time-effective way of communicating than the slow verbal system we use."

"I wonder if many people will believe you when you announce that pets communicate faster than humans?"

The idea of animals thinking faster than people obviously amused Chrissie. "I'm serious!" I said.

"Oh come on...you can't be."

"But I am, I tell you. Just think about this idea for a moment. Before you can say anything, you have to have a thought; and thoughts come from ideas in your mind."

"Alright, give me an example," she said, "and then I might understand more clearly."

"That's easy. Let's say that you see a man outside who's wearing a green hat and red shoes, and he's sporting a blue beard. What's the first thing you're going to notice about him?"

"The blue beard, I expect," she replied, grinning. "I don't see many men with blue beards around here."

"Right. So how would you draw my attention to what you've just seen?"

She thought for moment and then said, "There's a man outside with a blue beard."

"Ok. Before you put that thinking into words, you first had to have a picture in your mind; then you decided what you wanted to say. Next, you selected some words that best described what you wanted to say; and finally, you put the words into a sequence that created an intelligible sentence. You went through these steps in order to say what you wanted to tell me."

"Good heavens! Do I go through all of that every time I want to say something?"

"It gets even worse yet, Chrissie."

"How can it possibly get worse? I'm already tired...just wondering how I do it."

"Because the person you want to convey your message to has to hear the words, decipher the sounds, and convert them back into a picture."

"At this pace, I'm surprised that we ever get a conversation finished," she said, laughing.

"Especially when you won't stop long enough to listen," I chided.

I tried to avoid her smirk. "...just think for a moment. Your listener has heard your words but won't understand you until the words are changed back into a picture. The only words of value are man, blue beard, and outside. You expect your listener to know exactly what you are thinking with just three words."

"That could be difficult."

"It's impossible! The listener will create a vision of a man with a blue beard somewhere outside. The picture in your listener's mind is probably different to yours. Fortunately, most people have some intuition and will read your thoughts, which means they will interpret your 'thought pictures' and see more detail of what you are trying to say than your words express."

"I'm beginning to get the picture," said Chrissie, very aware of the pun.

"Animals' reactions are so much faster because they pass pictures to each other and don't waste time trying to convert a fraction of the picture to sound. In the wild, a faster reaction can mean the difference between life and death. Likewise, the difference between an ordinary sportsman and a great sportsman is the ability to read the thoughts, or pictures, put out by others."

"I'd never thought of this, Malcolm."

"It's true. Sportsmen who are able to lift themselves into the higher energy fields will have an advantage because they will know what the opposition is going to do a split second before it's actioned. A good competitor is always half a thought, or half a yard, ahead of rivals."

"This is all very interesting, but where's it getting us?"

Chrissie understood the explanation of communicating with pictures and was anxious to move on. "Your earlier question was about awareness in spirit. 'Does our awareness change?' I think you asked. To answer your question, yes, it does. We see and experience everything in pictures, and the pictures are in color, too."

Her wrinkled brow and pursed lips suggested that I needed to supplement my comments. "One of the drawbacks of humanity's becoming so intellectual, Chrissie, is that we have lost the art of thinking in pictures. In some ways, the Greeks and Phoenicians who developed phonetic writing around 2,000 B.C. did us a disservice. We remember more detail when we communicate in pictures."

"How can that be, Malcolm? This is fascinating."

"Ok, Chrissie, if I ask you to describe this room to me, or to write down what you see, you will recall only the basic and most important aspects of the room. However, if asked to draw a picture of this room, you will dig deeper into your picture world, even down to the patterns on the curtains. You would want to complete your picture."

"I think you're right."

"We cannot speak fast enough to say the words that we see in our pictures. The ancients who did not use written words had very good memory recall. They had to see what they wanted to pass on; and to be sure the other party was interpreting correctly, they had to give a complete and accurate picture."

"I've forgotten, Malcolm. Why are we discussing pictures versus words?"

"Because when we move into spirit, we move into picture thinking, which is the way of spirit communication."

"Oh…"

"As I've said, animals do it all the time. They give a more complete picture in less time than you communicate in words, Chrissie."

"How does that," she said, speaking slowly and trying to think the answer out as she phrased it, "help me find my own answers to those deep questions of spirituality?"

"Nothing is new, Chrissie. If I come up with novel ideas or new concepts, it's because I've reached into the higher dimensions and looked for them."

"But how do you do it?" she persisted.

"Remember what I said about not being in my body? The physical is something separate from me…something I use, not something I am."

"Yes, I remember."

"I can stay that way only if I remain free from the emotions that affect the body. Such states as anger and greed are expressions of physical emotions. They are no concern of the spiritual. What 'I do' is physical; what 'I am' is Love. In other words, Love is what I am. We've been through all this before."

"I do remember what you've told me, Malcolm."

"Reaching into the higher dimensions for information is just a matter of becoming one with the energy of the information I'm searching for, which is possible only if I stay separate from the energy of emotion that ties me to the physical body. Are you with me?"

"I'm not sure…"

"Think about emotion for a moment, Chrissie. With emotion, we build pictures and information that are based on emotional prejudice and bias. Emotion can change facts, blur the truth, to suit its own security or peace of mind."

"…sounds like something out of science fiction." She was struggling with the concept of all this.

"Chrissie, the spiritual world is a picture world. Everything you pray for has to be seen before it can be brought into being. As you become more able to dissolve emotion, free yourself from it, you won't have the clinging energy of that emotion to stop you from going through into the light. You've read about people who have been through near-death experiences?"

"Yes, I have."

"…how they say that their whole life flashes before their eyes?"

"Yes."

"Why do you think they say 'eyes'?"

"Hmm…because they saw images of their lives?"

"Brilliant, Chrissie! It is because they have experienced their life in picture form. What they 'see' during those moments are the passing emotions. Our memories are held in the emotions we have, which come back to us as pictures."

"From what I've read, some people see more pictures than others."

"That's right, Chrissie. With fewer emotions hanging around us, it's easier to leave our physical bodies and enter into the spiritual spheres."

"Is that how you anticipate what I'm going to say, or know what I'm thinking?"

"Yes. I can't read your mind, but I can 'see' the pictures you're thinking. Therefore, I see your thoughts faster than you can convert them to sound."

"Could I do that?" Chrissie asked, letting me know that she was really intrigued by all this.

"Of course you could, but start by seeing life in pictures. Try to see the pictures the animals are thinking, and then they will begin to see yours. You will be surprised how quickly animals will begin to respond."

"How do you know all of this, Malcolm?"

"Oh, Chrissie, I just do. I spent many happy years working with animals and learning to think in pictures. This gives me a greater degree of awareness because I see what others are thinking. Sometimes, it's called intuition. Often, I'm told I'm very perceptive. I just have a different base for awareness than most people."

"You want me to leave, don't you?" she asked, looking a bit hurt.

"I didn't say so."

"No, but I know you do. I can sense it." She stopped and thought before saying, "No, I can see it." She laughed.

"Chrissie, you're on your way to the exciting, more beautiful world of spiritual thinking."

"Thank you, Malcolm. I appreciate your encouragement."

"I know," I surprised her, "come back this afternoon when I have more time, and we'll carry on with this then."

Chrissie agreed. "I'll have some time to think about what you said so far," she added.

Later that afternoon, Chrissie asked, "I suppose you meditate," initiating our second discussion of the day.

"Why should you think that? I don't meditate at all."

For a moment or two, she was too shocked to think of anything to say. I smiled reassuringly and asked, "Why should I want to meditate? All it does is take you to the center of your thoughts, away from all the emotion you've created; but at some time, you have to come back through it and deal with the emotion. It isn't going to go away on its own, you know."

"I'm confused, Malcolm. I always thought you were a great believer in meditation."

"I am, providing we don't overdo it. Too much meditation could lead to the possibility of reaching a state where our minds would become permanently blank. We need to experience emotion but not become the emotion."

"How much is too much? How would I know?"

"It's easy to see when people have mediated beyond what's necessary for regaining composure. They have an empty look about them, as if there's no one inside to direct the body in its daily activities. In this state, people have difficulty interacting with emotions, theirs or other people's. It's a form of overdosing."

"So when should meditation be used?" Chrissie asked.

"…depends upon the individual; but if you use meditation to hold a picture in your mind and study it in detail, then you are getting somewhere."

"Should I meditate on a picture—not on a word or prayer?"

"Absolutely! That's right. With practice, it's possible to meditate on sound at the same time as you're becoming one with the picture."

"Really?"

"Yes, Chrissie. Some people see sound as shapes, and the design of the shape depends upon the sound. And, other people see color as shapes. It's just a matter of getting everything to harmonize, to effect the creation you want. You can also move to where you want to be through visualization, as you did when you were doing absent healing."

I could see that Chrissie was struggling to stay with me. "You'd better explain how you do that," she said, sighing slightly.

"…by bringing all the senses together in a single thought to create a picture. Meaning, I can smell what I hear, hear what I see, see what I smell, touch what I think, and so on. In spiritual terms, I can put together any combination of sensations. This is how great works of art come into creation."

"These thoughts are new to me," Chrissie said, encouraging me to continue.

"All inspirational works are visualized from the spiritual dimensions, and the energy of Love creates the image in solid form. We are just the pen in the hands of a spiritual master."

"You've explained so much!" Chrissie was excited. "I feel something of what you are saying when I'm lost in my art."

"Tell me what you mean."

"I remember one day when I started on a piece of sculpture. When I stopped working late in the evening, I realized that I had been sculpting for ten hours…hadn't been aware of anything during the whole time. I was completely caught up in my work; and when I finished, I stepped back and looked at the truly wonderful piece of art I'd produced. I know I can't repeat it—I wouldn't know how to begin."

I gave Chrissie an encouraging nod, and she continued, "During the hours I was creating, I became one with all my senses…was an amazing sensation."

"And I expect," I added, "that the finished sculpture is full of Love, a Love that can be touched, seen, and heard—an indescribable something."

"Exactly!" Chrissie was really excited because she was relating her love for art to our discussion.

"And did you meditate to reach that state?"

"No. I just became absorbed by it."

"If you had been meditating, you would have had the same sensations of peace and happiness during that wonderful time; but you wouldn't have produced anything. Meditation is preparation for something greater. It teaches you how to move to the center of your emotions; but once you can do that, you need to move into the Light."

Chrissie nodded in agreement. "Can you imagine living in that higher state permanently, Chrissie? It's possible once you've conquered all physical emotion. When you can do that, you will begin to see spiritual energy—be able to separate the energies in a single color and see all the colors in a single color. In that state, you will see the yellow of a flower in all the colors that create the yellow and the yellow in the same instant."

"Wow, Malcolm, I think you'd better back up and explain that one."

"Sure. When I move into that state, I see daffodils, for example, as a glorious, radiant yellow; but I also see the combinations of blues, reds, and greens in the petals in the same instant. I also feel the colors of the blossom—I am the flower."

"This is too much, Malcolm."

"That's just one example, Chrissie. Think about music. When I listen to great works of art in the music world, I see color, shapes, and smells in the music. I touch the music with my thoughts. It's a total experience, and I am the music. I blend with the energies causing the music to become the music. Energy that causes sound can be seen, so it must have shape and color. But, I can't be aware of any of this while locked into my physical emotions."

"Some people might say that is meditation," Chrissie said, testing me.

"We're discussing a state beyond meditation—it's living in this world with the Love sensations of the spiritual world. You have to move beyond meditation to create the beauty from another dimension in this Earthly world."

"Is that how you heal?" she asked.

"Yes. By eliminating the obstructive forces of negative emotion, I allow the spiritual energy that I am to move into this world. To reach that state, Chrissie, I have to eliminate the emotions that prevent my spirit of Love from coming through."

"How?"

"Healers can be unhappy or angry at times, just like everyone else. But when they start to heal, all of their emotions, such as anger, disappear immediately; and they become serene and relaxed until the healing is over. Then, they become emotional again. I've seen this many times."

"I'm thinking, Malcolm. Isn't activity of any sort the opposite of meditation?"

"Yes, it is. I separate from my emotions so that I can become the Love that I am. It's a different type of reality. Remember when you became so totally absorbed in your art? You separated from your emotions."

"Time passed quickly," Chrissie replied, recalling her earlier statements, "…hours seemed like minutes."

"No doubt, because time is just a measurement of energy flow. The faster your thoughts moved through the spiritual world, the faster you appeared to have moved on Earth; but, of course, your spirit was in the higher planes, not your body or emotions."

"Wait a sec…Malcolm. Can you go over this part again?"

"Ok. Let's take our conversation back to what I said about entering the center of your emotions. To move away from physical emotions and be spiritually aware, you need to reach a higher energy level. You do this by eliminating negative emotion—so that it doesn't interfere with spiritual energy, which is at a higher level. Then, you relay spiritual knowledge to the physical because there is no emotion to block it. You will have become the knowledge, assuming, of course, that you are Love. Anything less than Love will limit your awareness. For example, if you are bound to your possessions, like your jewelry, your fears and angers cause you to become a slave of emotion; and you cannot become spiritual. The only energy spirituality knows is Love."

"How long does it take, Malcolm, to move from a physical state to a spiritual state?"

"…instantaneous! I don't even think about it on a logical level. The spiritual state is my world—where I think from. Do you recall your first healing session? With the higher energy, I was able to separate you from your current emotions and to bring your past emotions to the surface. The emotions you experience create the block."

"So, really, I didn't go back to the past at all," she reasoned.

Chrissie was catching onto my thoughts now. "That's right," I confirmed, giving her a moment to process. I knew that she was moving through my energy and seeing the same pictures.

"You brought the past to me."

"I brought every emotion to you, knowing that the strongest and most distressing would surface easily. It was just a matter of waiting to see what surfaced. Emotion is only a form of memory, you know. Emotion is the substance around a memory. Release the emotion and the memory has no value. Hate is just a memory recall in action, and who wants to live in the past."

"Slow down!"

"As you wish, Chrissie. When you become your emotion, you live in the past—you cannot live in the spiritual world. The spiritual world is now. It's your awareness affected by whatever emotions you have around your memories. So you have two choices: live as a reflection of emotional yesterday; or be the Love you are now."

"You're too much, Malcolm. Can you remove emotion from everyone's memory?"

"Only if they want me to…most people want to keep their emotions and their memories. They want to be greedy, angry, etc. Most just aren't aware that there's an alternative."

A long silence followed as Chrissie thought over what had been said.

"I'm beginning to understand a bit more about what dying is all about," she said, speaking softly. "We are moving from the past to real awareness."

"Yes, you are understanding. When the body no longer has enough energy to hold the spirit, the spirit will move to the center of its emotions; and from there, it will pass through into the higher vibrations of the spiritual world. The emotions will have been left behind."

"What happens when you get there? Can you tell me this, Malcolm?"

"Let's stay with what's happening down here on Earth for a moment," I insisted. "Before you can fully appreciate the different energy levels in the spiritual world, you need to thoroughly understand them here."

"But…I need answers to so many questions."

"All in good time. I promise you. One of the most important things I can teach you here is to conquer your negative emotions. It's essential to spiritual development to become the Love I keep talking about. Anything less than total Love will hold you to the lower vibrations of matter, here and in the next dimension."

"Hmm…"

"Chrissie, Why would we want to live or experience life as a memory? This is what happens when we become so emotional—when we have become locked into our past and have stopped experiencing the now. If we could let go of the past and all the emotions associated with it, we could be permanently spiritual…be the experience of Love, which is a natural and different state from fear."

"What?"

"All fear is based on memory recall brought to life by emotion."

"I need to meditate on this," a smiling Chrissie said, getting up to leave. "It's a film I will have to meditate on, not just a picture."

I smiled. She was setting me up for the next round.

Hesitating at the door, Chrissie turned and said, "I'll see you next week, Malcolm, after I've had some time to sort this all out in my head. Get the picture?"

Chapter Eleven
LOVE, TO BE OR DESTROY

"I think we'd better call this your Chrissie Day," Debbie said, smiling. "I've never known anyone with so many questions."

"...and so eager to ask them! Nothing stops Chrissie. Is she here, already, this early?"

"Yes, and about as excited as she can get. Do you want me to put something in her coffee to calm her down?" Debbie laughed and turned to listen to messages on the answer phone.

"That machine is a contradiction in terms," I said, going through to the treatment room.

"What, the answering machine? Why?"

"Because it never answers anything. Try phoning someone and asking their answer machine a question."

"Perhaps I should think pictures to it," Debbie said, chuckling as she closed the door.

"...morning Chrissie. So what are we discussing today?"

"Can we just clear up some of the points you've raised during the past few weeks?"

"Of course...the first one?"

"I understand now what you mean when you say, 'Love is who your *are*.'" But, I'm not sure how to get to that state. How will I know when I am Love?"

"You will never know, Chrissie. Other people will know."

"What good is this Love to me if I don't know about it?" she asked, sounding disappointed.

"Come on Chrissie, the Love you are is not for you. We've been through all this before."

"Yes, but…"

"There are no but's. Once you become Love, you will never again feel hurt, abused, or fearful. Life will take on a whole new meaning. You will become the awareness of Love and know beauty in the depths of despair—the despair of others, that is. You will have lifted beyond emotions or despair; and in that state, you will be able to lift others from their despair into your Love. Empathy doesn't mean going down to someone—it means raising them up to be one in your happiness."

"How do you do that?"

"You're not listening, Chrissie. I'll teach you how to listen one day when we have time."

"That wasn't very nice," she replied, sounding peevish. "I'm trying to learn."

"Ok, but your last question caused me to realize that you still haven't fully appreciated that Love doesn't *do* anything. You asked, 'How do you *do* that?'"

"…and I was serious."

"When people are in the depths of despair, I don't *do* anything. If someone comes to me feeling depressed, sad, in pain, grieving, or worse, I don't *do* anything. I certainly don't feel sympathy, pity, or even concern for them."

"Oh, but you do! I've seen you help people."

"No, Chrissie, I'm just there, as a spiritual healer, and making Love available. Many people are spiritual healers but don't know they're healers because they don't *do* anything specifically."

"Like nurses?" she asked, smiling. "…grandmothers?"

"Yes, that's right. Those lovely angels have learnt that empathy lifts the sick and suffering into their world of happiness, joy, and contentment, rather than taking themselves down into the other's world of fear, pain, and anxiety."

"Malcolm, surely we are allowed to feel sorry for someone."

Chrissie was still wanting to *do* something. "No, Chrissie. People in need of help are already surrounded by people who feel sorry for them. What good does it do? Believe me, feeling sorry does no good at all. Anyway, the suffering certainly don't want you to add negative attitudes to their problems."

"So what could I do to help?"

"There you go again…using the *do* word."

"Really Malcolm, if someone needed help, I couldn't just stand by and *do* nothing." Her agitation was surfacing.

"Yes, you can, Chrissie; but if you really need to fit a *do* into Love, lift the suffering up into your world of happiness by letting them become one with the Love you *are*."

Chrissie thought for a minute or two before a smile brightened her face. "Yes, I remember Grandmom used to do that when I was unhappy; she still does it, even now. When I'm depressed or sad, I always go to Grandmother. She doesn't do or say anything. She gives me that beautiful smile of hers; and, somehow, everything seems better. When she smiles, I just know that everything will be just fine."

"Does she sympathize with you?" I asked.

"Chrissie was silent for a few seconds before replying, "I don't think she ever has. When I think about it, she's never been unhappy for me. Even when I was in such a state about the abortion, Grandmom was all love, and smiles. She didn't offer any advice. She was there; and, somehow, her presence was enough. It gave me the strength to deal with the problem myself."

"See what I mean? Chrissie, Love isn't what you *do*, it's what you *are*. It's being calm and Loving without pity or sympathy. Grandmother's Love and calmness gave you the strength to lift yourself out of your problem state; sympathy would have confined you in it. One is what you *are*; the other is what you *do*."

"This is a bit difficult," Chrissie persisted, "so here's my next question. How do I become Love?"

"You've asked a difficult question, Chrissie, which cannot be answered in one set way. Love begins to happen when you want it and know how to pray or ask for Love to help you…to help you eliminate negative emotions from your thoughts."

"…begins to happen? What do I do to start? Help me with this one, Malcolm."

"I suppose the first step is to realize that you have chosen whatever emotion you feel. If you feel hurt by what someone said to you or about you, it's because you have chosen to feel hurt. You could just as easily have ignored what was said. No one hurts you or makes you feel sad. You choose to be negative."

"Now, Malcolm, if someone says something terrible about me, how can I stop myself from feeling hurt or angry?"

"At first, you may feel anger or hurt in your thoughts; but listen to what you are thinking and feeling and change your thoughts and feelings. By doing this, you will realize that you could just as easily ignore the negative remarks made about you."

"This may require some practice!"

"…shouldn't, Chrissie. What others say or do becomes a problem only when you listen or accept. If someone has negative thoughts about you, they must be hurting for some reason. If someone tries to annoy you in some way, or feels you have annoyed them, because of something you innocently said or did, ignore the whole situation. Such matters become problems only when you accept them into your thoughts. When you are free of negative emotion, people will be unable to control you."

"Really?"

"Yes. Once someone works out your negative response attitudes, they will use them to control you. If you are free of negative attitudes, you cannot be controlled by others. You become free!"

"…sounds right," Chrissie reasoned, "but what if someone said something really, really terrible about you? Wouldn't you feel hurt or anger towards them? Wouldn't you want to put the record straight? Surely you would want to defend yourself?"

"Why? Chrissie? If I'm happy with me, what is there to say? If I fought back, defended myself, I would hurt someone. Love doesn't *do* anything. It certainly doesn't hurt others in defense of itself."

"You sure can turn my thoughts around—that's just the opposite of what I would've thought, Malcolm."

"…being able to totally accept yourself, as you are. Once you can do this, other people's thoughts about you are unimportant, provided, of course, you are not being deliberately malicious. If you were, Love would be very distant from who you *are*."

"I'm with you so far, Malcolm, but what about the defense of others?"

Chrissie was really chewing on this bone, and I resolved to be patient. "…depends on the situation," I replied. If someone is being critical of another who is absent, suggest that they wait until the other person is present. Don't get involved. If someone is being slandered, refuse to give the negative remarks credibility."

"How does Love enter into this scenario?"

"Love usually prevails. Anger, hurt, and other emotions soften or change in the presence of Love."

She wasn't finished. "What would you do if you saw someone being physically abused?" she asked, determined that I wouldn't avoid this point.

"Alright, Chrissie, let's go to the extreme. You are really asking, 'Would I kill to protect innocence?'"

"I suppose I am," she agreed.

"The answer? I would. Have you heard the old saying, 'Too many good people have died because too many good people did nothing?'"

"Yes, and it can be so true," she said, nodding.

"If I had the means of preventing a killing by taking the life of the one responsible, and if that were the only way, I would kill.

But I wouldn't do it with emotion—not with anger, sadness, or satisfaction. I would kill only to protect Love. We've discussed this before; it's the emotion behind the action or thought that is all important."

"I'll have to give these points some serious consideration Malcolm. At the moment, I can't fully comprehend the thought of killing without having emotions."

"Love is a strength, Chrissie—it's not weak. There are times when it has to stand up and say what needs to be said, at the risk of causing others to turn against it. Love is not about being popular—it's about truth. In this example, we're talking about being Love in the midst of hate, absorbing hate, and replacing it with Love. The same applies to all negative emotions. Love does nothing to gain support or followers; Love has no interest in power. Love just is."

"Oh, Malcolm, you make all this sound so simple, and I could listen to your explanations forever. However, you still haven't answered my question."

"Which question?"

"How do I, Chrissie, become Love?"

"Oh, yes. Rid yourself of fear."

"…another simple-sounding answer, which could take a lifetime to achieve!"

"Not really, Chrissie, if you develop the right attitudes. We've already discussed fear of death. Now, begin to work towards being free of all fear."

"Considering the world we live in, is this advice really practical?" she asked, allowing her thoughts to surface. "I mean, if someone says they are going to physically hurt me, I'm bound to be frightened."

"In your scenario, you'd be experiencing an emotion before the event; and this is more likely to ensure that you would be hurt, rather than preventing the person from hurting you. Fear attracts fear. I'm not saying you should enjoy being hurt; but it's less likely to happen if you have no fear of being hurt. Believe me, Chrissie, if you picture yourself being hurt, losing your home, or any other frightening incidents, you are creating the events in your mind; and this can cause them to happen, because you are creating energy with your thoughts of fear. The energy you create will attract more fear energy to itself and will grow."

"So, people can create their own hurt?"

"Fear is a very powerful emotion, as are guilt, hate, jealousy, etc. To become Love, free yourself of negative emotions."

"This question may seem redundant to you, Malcolm, but what other emotions must I release or avoid?"

"Free yourself of wanting or possessiveness. You cannot possess people or objects. If you feel you cannot let go of something, you have made a god of it. There's nothing or no one you can call your own. If you feel that an object or a person is more important to you than anything else, you are being possessive. Even your Love is not your Love—you cannot know of it until someone has received it. Possessiveness is linked to jealousy, envy, and selfishness."

"Explain," Chrissie said, sighing to let me know that my last response had been a little long and overwhelming.

"Through wanting, Chrissie. If you really want something, you can manifest it; but are you depriving someone else? Both wanting and possessiveness get in the way of Love. Think for a moment. What in this vast world could I give you, Chrissie, that would make you a better person than you are? What could I take from you that would cause you to be a lesser person than you are?"

She shrugged her shoulders. "The answer to both questions is 'nothing.' You are the sum of your thoughts, not your possessions. Remember who you *are*. You can become greed just as easily as you can become fear, hate, or Love."

"Should I give away what I have, if I have more than others?"

"Certainly not, Chrissie. Now you are suggesting gross irresponsibility. If someone has a lot of money or possessions, which they came by honestly, their wealth is a gift, like having an artistic talent is a gift. It's what they do with the gift that is all important. You could use your artistic talent to promote or paint perverted art just as a wealthy person could use their money adversely. In either case, activities lacking Love will hold the one with the gifts in lower, baser, spiritual energies when they move to the next world."

Knowing that Chrissie was relating my comments to her artistic talent, I sat quietly for moment. I wanted to give her time to absorb the points about possessiveness before changing the topic. "Finally, Chrissie," I continued, "we need to be free of superiority."

"Here we go again! I don't think I'm very superior."

Her voice lacked its usual serious tone, and I sensed that her attention was ebbing. So I quickly moved forward. "When you realize that every life—every bird, animal, insect, and plant—has the same energy as yourself, you can know in your heart that you are as dependent upon them as they are upon you. When you know that we are all bound to and part of the same Love, you will have become that Love."

"Sorry to be such a bore," she said, expressing her lack of understanding, "but how will I know?"

"When you reach the Love state, Chrissie, the world around you will seem changed. For example, during walks in the woods or fields, birds and animals will continue around you as if you are not there."

"But they're wild. How would birds and animals accept me?"

"With Love. If you have no fear, they will not detect fear in you and will feel safe. If you have fear in your thoughts, wildlife will stay away. Fear means danger, and wildlife does not want to be involved in your danger."

"Sounds wonderful."

"Life can be wonderful, Chrissie, if we are free of possessiveness. Just like with fear, wildlife will stay away if you have possessiveness in your heart. The wild ones, as you referred to them, do not want to be possessed. The plant and animal kingdoms want to remain free, as all Love wants to be free."

"But humans just tend to think they are superior," she reminded me.

"Well, as with fear and possessiveness, wildlife will detect a sense of superiority, thoughts of control and domination that are linked to power, and will avoid you. Wildlife wants to be free and share the beauty of Love. Fear, possessiveness, and superiority destroy Love."

Her deep sigh let me know that she was evaluating her own emotions. "If you are able to be free of fear, possessiveness, and superiority," I continued, "wildlife will hardly notice your presence."

"Would birds and little animals really come up to me if I became total Love?" she asked softly. "That would be wonderful. I think the most wonderful thing I've ever experienced is being trusted by a wild bird. A little speckled bird comes to my window every day to be fed and now trusts me enough to eat out of my hand. Having this bird trust me is the most wonderful thing I've known."

"So you know what I mean?"

"Oh, yes, I do. You must be in paradise when you sit in a field and have deer, rabbits, birds, and butterflies come and play around you."

"We can take this even further, Chrissie. Once you become the Love that I keep going on about, the animals and other life will let you become one with them. Instead of just watching, you'll find that you can buzz around as a bumble bee; or you can become one with a bird and take flight."

"That would be great."

"Just as you became one with your sculptures, so you could become one with any of the life your Love harmonizes with. All it takes is to be free of negative emotions and to realize that Love just is."

"Is that what you meant when you said I wouldn't know my own Love until it was reflected back?"

"Did I say that?"

"You know you did, Malcolm!"

"Yes, Chrissie, the best way I can describe Love is to say that it's like the light shining from a candle. A candle's light can only travel away from the center of the flame; and as it travels into the darkness, it gives warmth to those who are drawn to its light."

"A beautiful image…"

"It's true. Love, as light, must forever travel away from its source. It can't return to the flame that gave it life. This is why I say you cannot know your own Love and that there is nothing you can do with it. Your Love has left you and been taken up by another before you are aware of its presence."

"Your descriptions make me want to just hold Love in my hands, like a bird."

"Sorry, Chrissie, we can't own or hold the Love, or light, that comes from another. We can bathe in its warmth, reflect in its light, and rejoice in its beauty; but we cannot *do* anything with it."

"Seems to me that we should be able to know our own Love," Chrissie said, looking at the clock on the wall. "Somehow, it's all a bit sad."

"Light, Love, travels away from the flame, the spirit, that brings it to life. You can't know of light that travels away from you, and if you try to hold it to yourself, light will go out."

"Geez, Malcolm, I thought I asked a simple question," she said, walking toward the door.

"Come on, Chrissie, brighten up, or I will have to turn the lights on."

"Sorry," she said, "my candle was reflecting on what you said."

She gave me a big smile and went out into the day. Or, I thought she had. The door opened moments later, and Chrissie's lovely face reappeared. She smiled and said: "Can I ask just one more quick question?"

"How quick?" I asked.

"I never know when I ask a question if it's going to require a long answer or a short one," she replied.

"Does this mean that your next question is complex?"

"Oh, no," she said, with a mischievous grin. By now, she had seated herself again. My questions are quite straightforward; it's the answers that seem to be complex."

"Let's have it," I said, "and I hope it requires a short answer because it's nearly time you weren't here. So there isn't time for a lengthy answer, Chrissie."

"Oh, I forgot," she said, grinning from ear to ear. "Debbie asked me to tell you that the next client had to reschedule."

"She did, did she?" I'll have to have a word with Debbie."

"I've been wondering for a long time," Chrissie continued, "how Love can make whole again Love damaged by malice or greed."

"Oh Chrissie, what sort of question is that? You must have been thinking that one up for weeks."

"No, not necessarily in recent weeks, Malcolm. This question has intrigued me ever since I was a little girl. I've wanted to know what happens to people who are killed—what happens when they reach heaven. I've wondered what state their spirit is in when they reach the other side. If they die in great pain or distress, how are they healed?"

"Alright, Chrissie, but a big part of your question will be answered when we have discussed enough about becoming Love during earthly life and move on to a discussion of the spiritual world."

"I'm looking forward to that, but it's like waiting for tomorrow. Tomorrow is always as far away as ever."

"I know…be patient."

"If you insist…Malcolm."

"Now, about God healing those who have suffered or been killed. As I said earlier, anyone who kills or hurts another must first destroy that part of their own Love that would have prevented the killing; and because they are responsible for the destruction of their own Love, they must go on to make themselves whole again.'

"I remember this part."

"Good. However, those who have suffered through no fault of their own are taken into special receiving homes in the next world where they can spend from weeks to months, in earthly time asleep while God's healing Love makes them whole again."

"How does God do that?" Chrissie was back in her rhythm of asking questions.

"By taking to Himself all the hurt, pain, and sorrow inflicted on those who have become Love."

"Sounds simple enough, but…"

"It is beyond comprehension, Chrissie, to imagine the agony that the Greatest Love takes to itself in order to make whole again damaged Love. The sadness and suffering that Love absorbs to ensure the continued peace and spiritual enlightenment of those who have remained true to the laws of Love is incredible."

I paused, giving Chrissie some time to think. When she gave me a reassuring glance, I continued, saying, "That is why it is so important that we all free ourselves of the emotions of hate, anger, etc. When we hurt another, including the innocence of the animal world as well, we are inflicting pain on the Love that gives us life and awareness. Eventually, we must all take back to ourselves the pain or suffering that we have caused in another. All the emotions of suffering, no matter how small, must eventually be taken back to ourselves so that we can advance spiritually."

"Wow, Malcolm, all debts must be paid."

"Right. Sooner or later, everybody will come into the light of Love."

"Some people must have a lot of sadness awaiting them," Chrissie said with a serious tone. "I'm thinking about those who kill or hurt others in the name of their god. Seemingly, you're saying that killing or hurting another in the name of religion, or religious ideology, causes God the greatest hurt."

"Yes, that's right, Chrissie. Just thinking about it makes me sad. People kill or abuse others in the name of their god without realizing that they are causing the Greatest of Love the greatest of suffering. Eventually, they will come to know of the hurt they have caused, and their grief will be beyond measurement. Those who fight, or cause suffering in some way, in the name of Love, or the leader or prophet they honor, are in fact doing their chosen Love the greatest harm."

"Why is that?" She had settled into a quiet mood.

"Because anyone hurt in the name of Love will be made whole by the Love, which they were hurt for."

"Can you say that again?" Chrissie asked. "Only I want to know what you really mean by this."

"Sure. Let us say someone on Earth says he doesn't agree with me. That's alright by me. As I've said many times, in many ways, no one can abuse me unless I agree to be abused; and I have chosen any emotion I have. I could choose happiness in place of anger, or Love in place of hurt."

"I remember," Chrisse said, moving from her chair and onto the floor. She glanced my way, giving me a signal to continue.

"I don't mind if someone disagrees with me and is vocal about it. They are free to choose their emotions, as I am mine. For our example, however, suppose that another person gets upset because I do nothing about the vocal one. So out of support for me, my defender attacks with aggressive, negative words and hurts the person who disagreed with me."

"I understand," Chrissie said thoughtfully. "The person who disagreed with you was hurt by the person who supported you."

"That's right. How do you think I feel about it all? I feel terrible. The spiritual hurt going through me will be more than equal to the hurt the one who has suffered can know. The thought of one soul suffering in my name is unthinkable; I wish no one to defend me. I'm not concerned about what others do or think; but if someone should cause hurt by defending me, I have to put it right."

"Is that why Jesus was so distressed when one of the disciples attacked a soldier who had come for Jesus?"

"Of course it was, Chrissie, and now you know why Jesus made the soldier whole again."

"Yes, I understand."

"If I can feel distress at the thought of someone being hurt in my defense, think how much more the hurt, the suffering, must be in the heart of the Greatest Love. It's terrible to think of all the suffering and hurt being absorbed by the Greatest Love, prophets, and other Loving souls just because people are defending in their names, or hurting and killing in their names. Those who are hurt or killed will quickly forget their pain because the Greatest Love, for whom they were hurt or killed, will absorb their pain and suffering."

"That's just awesome, Malcolm!" said a wide-eyed Chrissie, sitting on the floor with legs crossed.

"...and when those who are, or have been, responsible for destroying Love come to realize what they have done, they will go down on their knees and beg forgiveness in their distress. Forgiveness will come only when they take back to themselves the hurt they caused."

"I'm glad I returned, Malcolm, and that we continued this discussion. I'm feeling inspired."

"Wonderful, Chrissie. When anyone hurts Love and unnecessarily causes harm to any form of life, they cause pain and suffering in the Love of all Love and must eventually know it for themselves."

"People who go out hunting and killing should feel a bit insecure."

"Yes, they should. Saying 'I didn't know' won't do much good. In our hearts, we know when we are doing harm to other life, to satisfy selfish emotion."

Silence fell over us for a moment. No doubt, Chrissie was thinking about her own emotions, and past thoughts and actions.

"Of course," I said, interrupting the silence, "some of those who say they have been hurt or abused may not be included in this spiritual law because they could have chosen to ignore or to be another emotion."

"Malcolm, all of this is terribly sad and beautiful at the same time. To think that God would suffer for me even if I haven't fully accepted Him is beautiful. How could I not accept the beauty of Love, knowing this, and do all I can to get rid of other emotions."

"I think we've discussed enough for today, don't you, Chrissie?"

"Please, can I ask just one more…a very quick one?"

"Alright, Chrissie, but do make it a quick one."

"I was just wondering…how can you tell if someone is the Love you talk about, or if they're expressing just a passing emotion?"

I contained my smile. Chrissie obviously had someone in mind. "By the eyes, Chrissie. The eyes never lie. By looking into a person's eyes, you will see what their spiritual worth has become. You will quickly learn to recognize whether someone is Love, or perhaps hate, fear, possessiveness, jealousy, or superiority. Whatever a person has become will shine through their eyes. What they are can't be hidden, not even for a second."

"I must train myself to look at eyes," she thought aloud.

"Take care, though, for hate would sooner destroy the light of Love than be forced into brightness. Love should never be forced into anyone's life. Everyone must search and strive to become Love in their own way, in their own time."

"Now, Chrissie, it really is time you went along."

Chapter Twelve
TO LIVE OR DIE

"Hi Chrissie. Where have you been? We haven't seen you for several weeks."

Gone was the bright, effervescent personality I had known earlier. The Chrissie who walked into my office was carrying some heavy burden that was taking her strength and making demands on her happiness and freedom of spirit. She didn't speak right away. She came in and took her usual place in the armchair by my desk. After a few moments of silence, her eyes turned down; and I could feel her aloneness.

"It's Grandmom…" she said, so softly that I heard her thoughts more clearly than her words.

At such times, words have no place, no meaning; and anyway, she wouldn't have heard them. Chrissie was in a place of her own making. The Chrissie we had come to know and love wasn't present. I was observing a shadow of the former Chrissie.

"The past few weeks have been terrible," she said, having difficulty starting her story. "I went over to see Grandmom one evening and knew as I walked through the door that something was wrong. I could feel it, or rather couldn't feel it. The house felt empty, as if I had walked into the past. Oh, Malcolm, it was so weird. I felt like I had walked into a dream; I became lost in the past. I can't describe how I felt…I wasn't there, but I was. As I walked through the rooms, something clutched my heart…something had its fingers around my throat, and my eyes were seeing fear."

She paused and looked at me, as if seeking encouragement to continue. I nodded.

"I was held in this unreal world until I walked into Grandmom's room. She was lying on the bed as she often was, and as I walked in, she turned to look at me. In that instant, reality took hold of me again; and I realized that Grandmom was very sick. She didn't say anything, but the way she looked at me…her eyes said it all. I sensed the relief she felt."

"What did you do after you realized that her condition was so serious?"

"I just looked at her and asked, 'Grandmom, why didn't you call me? What's wrong?'"

Chrissie reached for the tissue box. "Grandmom told me she knew I was coming and that she didn't want me to change my plans for her. 'I could wait,' she said. My heart was aching as I dialed 911. The ambulance came right away, and the paramedics told me that Grandmom had suffered a stroke. They took her to the hospital and that's when it all began."

"Please tell me what happened," I prompted, even though I already knew. I'd been through these situations many, many times.

Chrissie continued as if I hadn't said anything. "She was in a ward with others…no privacy…the drugs…the injections…the tests. Somehow, it was all so degrading, in comparison to the independent life she'd lived. Please don't misunderstand me. The nurses were wonderful. They must be angels to do the things they do, with such compassion. But…why couldn't they just let her go?"

At this, Chrissie broke down. I sat quietly as she cried and released some of her emotions. After she composed herself, she continued. "Grandmom had a stroke. Her vision had been deteriorating quickly; and after the stroke, she could hardly see at all. Her left side was most affected. Everything that was necessary for her happiness had gone. If she had lived, she would have been totally dependent on others. She would have hated that. Malcolm, she was eighty-eight, and the doctors tried every way they could think of for over two weeks to keep her alive. What I can't understand is, why?"

Knowing that Chrissie wasn't quite finished, I did not respond to her question. She restated it. "I know that doctors have to do these things; they think it's their responsibility to keep people alive. But is it?"

"What do you think?"

"She was an elderly lady who couldn't see or hear well, and she was probably in pain. But worst of all, Grandmom was unable to attend to the functions of life for herself. To me, keeping her alive was wrong, when all she wanted to do was die. Several times, she whispered to me, 'Please, Chrissie, tell them to let me go…no more, please.'"

Silence fell upon us for a moment as Chrissie drew a deep breath and sighed. "No one listened to Grandmom," she said, expressing deep sadness. "I remember what you said about being prepared to let others help you—not thinking of yourself as a burden; but surely it can't be right to keep someone in Grandmom's condition alive."

"You've raised a big, important question, Chrissie," I said, "and I agree. In a situation such as your Grandmother's, all that is required is Love; and when Love is not sufficient to hold someone in this world, have enough Love in your heart to let Love go."

"Love…"

"This principle doesn't apply only to the elderly, Chrissie. It applies to all levels of life. The time comes, sometimes it's obvious and other times not, when Love needs to take over and say, 'No more!' Provided every possible means is being taken to reduce pain and suffering, the time comes when all one can do, or should do, is to rely on the power of Love. Love can determine where awareness should continue."

"Do you believe in euthanasia, Malcolm?"

Chrissie was returning. The Love that she was had traveled with Grandmom to help her through her emotion and into the next world. As often happens, Chrissie's spirit hadn't wanted to return and had become lost in the emotional depths of her Grandmother's thoughts. This sometimes happens; and when it does, Love needs help from this side to find its way back. This is a big part of a healer's work.

"No, Chrissie, I do not believe in euthanasia. But as I have said, I think it's equally wrong to hold a spirit to a body when the spirit's time has come to go. Just as it's wrong to unnecessarily induce a birth, so it's equally wrong to induce a death. Strict spiritual laws govern both birth and death; and if we are to proceed in the proper way, Love must be given every chance to ease the way."

"Is speeding up the dying process a sin?"

"…depends on what you mean by 'speed up.' Deliberately taking the life of another is always wrong, even if they ask for that help. Though it is not wrong to withhold the means by which they are being kept alive."

Chrissie didn't respond, so I continued, "I have seen several people die, Chrissie; and in every case, the spirit of the body had left its shell before the body had taken its last breath."

"You mean a breathing body can be empty of spirit?" whispered Chrissie, as if afraid of awakening some imaginary body.

"Yes, that is absolutely right. As soon as there is insufficient energy in the body to restrain the spirit, the spirit moves away from the body in which it has been experiencing life. However, the spirit cannot go far, Chrissie. It cannot journey to the center of its emotion and into the light until the electromagnetic attraction that the body has for it is finally broken…that only happens when all energy expires from the body."

"So, Malcolm, you're telling me that Grandmom wasn't suffering in that final week when she was unconscious, aren't you?" Chrissie now sounded more like the Chrissie we knew—happy and excited.

"Right, Chrissie, Grandmother probably left the body almost as soon as she got to the hospital."

"But she kept waking," Chrissie said, "and whispering to me."

"…only for a few seconds or a minute or so at a time, right?"

"Yes," Chrissie said, thinking carefully. "She always went right back to sleep after waking for a moment."

"She wasn't sleeping, Chrissie. Grandmom would have been out of her body and watching the events from a safe distance. I suspect she was very annoyed as she watched the doctors trying to keep her body going, when she no longer had use of it. That's why she whispered to you and let you know that she just wanted to go."

"Would she have felt any pain or discomfort, Malcolm?"

"None at all except for those brief moments when she reentered her body to speak with you. Her biggest problem would have been frustration with the doctors who were doing their best at logical and medical levels. At a spiritual level, they were completely messing it up."

"Oh, if only I could be sure you are right," Chrissie said, sighing. "It would be such a comfort to know that she hadn't suffered."

"Nearly twenty years ago, Chrissie, I was suddenly taken very seriously ill. I was in excruciating pain in every muscle of my body. The pain was so intense I decided to leave my body. I didn't enter it again for three days and did so only when I heard two nurses discussing my condition. One nurse said to the other that the doctors thought all of my pain had gone. After hearing this remark, I decided to reenter my body. The nurse was quite right. My body was pain free, so I was quite happy to stay in it. That experience taught me how to leave my body whenever it suits me, which sometimes can be quite useful."

"That's incredible, Malcolm. Are you saying all people could leave their bodies if they knew how?"

"No, not everyone; but those who have managed to eliminate the negative emotions have the least difficulty. As I've said, emotion hangs like a fog about us and hold us to itself, but any form of shock can cause us to 'flip out.'"

"But everyone leaves their body before it stops breathing, is that right?"

Chrissie was back in form. "No, not everyone, Chrissie. People who have a fear of death will struggle to stay with a body that's trying to reject them. If only people would accept the inevitable, there would be no suffering in death. Unfortunately, our modern system of care adds to the suffering. By trying to keep people alive artificially on drugs and technology, we have developed the suggestion, or created the belief, that there is something wrong about dying; and so we try to stay alive forever. Staying healthy is different from hanging on to this life when our time has come to make the transition. When we are free of the negative emotions, we can remain healthy to the end and die peacefully."

"When some people are dying, they seem to stay conscious and aware until the end. Why is that, Malcolm, if their spirit has already gone?"

"The subconscious of the body is so well programmed that it will keep playing the program that's in the brain, even after the spirit has left. That is how the martyrs of old were able to sing and pray and appear to be without pain while burning to death. They had programmed themselves with such fervor and faith that their bodies continued to play the program long after they had departed the body. For the majority of people, they will have left their body hours or days before their final breath."

"I feel so relieved, Malcolm, knowing that my lovely Grandmom was in a safe place and watching over us."

After a momentary pause, Chrissie came back with, "But you still haven't explained why it's so terribly wrong to end life prematurely."

"If we do it ourselves, Chrissie, we must be reborn to complete what we ended prematurely. That's a spiritual law. If the reason was unselfish and the death very near the end of life expectancy, the spirit goes to a place of rest where it can recover. If, however, the reason was selfish, like a suicide to escape a responsibility, the spirit, when free of the body, wanders in a loneliness of grayness until the full span of its life expectancy is completed. At that time, the spirit will reenter the world of light."

Realizing that we had departed from our topic, I said, "I think we should return to this matter later."

"Oh, why can't we do it now? Why do you always save the best parts for later?"

"Because this subject fits in with what I want to tell you when we get to a discussion of life in the spiritual realms. I have to maintain some structure in what I'm telling you, Chrissie, or we will be hopping all over the place."

"Oh, come on, Malcolm, just once, break the rules and tell me what really happens when someone commits suicide."

"Well, alright, just this once, Chrissie, I'll ignore my rules—just for you. When a person, a spirit of Love, allows emotion to start dictating their attitudes, they begin to lose control of their own destiny. When Love gives way to anger, hate, or self-pity, as in this case, it allows a fog of emotion to form around the physical mind, which makes it increasingly difficult for the spirit of Love to get through; and there are always spirits around that have not made it to the spiritual spheres, because they've become the hate or selfishness I mention so often. These spirits are drawn to the atmosphere or emotion of hate, self-pity, etc., which they have become; and they begin to act out their own emotions through the human forms of others."

"There you are!" said Chrissie, as if she had just guided me through a surgical operation. "Was that so bad? Don't stop now, Malcolm, keep talking."

I couldn't help smiling because of her humor, knowing she had sidetracked me into giving her a preview of where all the talk of Love was eventually going to head. "Ok," I said. "I'll finish this bit, now that I've started."

"Please do."

"If people begin to feel sorry for themselves and sink into the depths of self-pity or just lack the spiritual courage to face up to their responsibilities, they will be handing themselves over, in a manner of speaking, to the loveless and perverted spirits of the darker world."

"You mean that darker spirits can actually influence our thinking?"

"That's right, Chrissie. In the spiritual world of Love, we refer to them as shades, because they move around in dark places. As I said, their home is in the darker regions. They are drawn by emotions such as lust and anger to whatever it is that attracts them and then they get into the emotional field of those who are developing perverted or unspiritual emotions. Shades use powerful thought images to make the person who is turning from Love act out their own disgusting desires. In this way, shades satisfy their base emotions."

"Now that's really scary!" she said, looking horrified.

"It is very scary, Chrissie. People have no idea how they are being used by other thought forms—just because they prefer self, ego, or some other negative or perverted emotion to Love."

"So what happens to the suicides?" Chrissie hadn't finished chewing on this bone yet.

"Once shades recognize an emotional weakness, and in the case of suicide it is to escape responsibility, they begin to plague the mind of the one who is developing the emotion of self-pity. To understand this fully, we must see it from the spiritual side. A power game is taking place between the purity or strength of Love on this side and sadistic pleasure on the other. Love is all that can save someone who has allowed such base emotions to take over, Chrissie."

"But how does suicide…"

"No one ever takes their own life without help—they are talked into it by shades of another world," I responded, before

Chrissie finished her question.

"Believe me. When we have discussed every aspect of Love from the human side, we will move to the various emotional states, as I know them from the perspective of the spiritual world."

"I can hardly wait!" Chrissie's imagination was now running in overdrive. "How much do I have to learn about Love before we can start to explore this other world?" she asked, barely able to contain her excitement.

"…depends on how many questions you ask."

Chapter Thirteen
ABILITY

"You look brighter than the last time I saw you, Chrissie."

She was wearing bright, happy colors and was obviously her usual cheerful self again.

"I know," she replied, smiling widely, "it was so weird how I just couldn't pull myself together after Grandmom's death. When I look back, it all seems so unreal. Do you know what I mean?" She didn't wait for an answer. In her mind, she hadn't asked a question.

One of the lovely things about Chrissie was that most of the questions she asked didn't require answers. Her mind moved so fast that it couldn't stop long enough to remember it had asked a question. As she chatted on, I heard myself thinking that I must teach this girl to listen to herself.

I suddenly realized I wasn't listening to Chrissie, either. Part of my awareness was with a person at distance who had called earlier and asked for absent healing. I quickly turned my attention back to what she was telling me—something about a cousin and stress.

"Sorry Chrissie, I said. "Can you go over that again? I missed the point of what you were telling me."

She looked at me quietly for a moment or two. "Are you alright?" she asked, expressing concern.

"Yes. Perfectly. Why?"

"Seems like you have something on your mind. I could come back another time, if you'd like. I don't mind, Malcolm, really."

"No…just having a passing thought. I'm fine. Thanks for asking, Chrissie."

"As you wish," she said, "but I still don't think you're totally with me."

"Up to a point, you're right. I'm with a man who is terminally ill, and I promised to stay with him spiritually and to help him to the other side. The time is nearly here, so part of me is helping him, with Love, to find his way to the Light."

"Can you tell me how you do that? Oops! I shouldn't use the *do* word, should I?" She gave me one of her funny Chrissie looks.

"That's ok, Chrissie. I know what you mean. Ask this question next week, though, would you? You were mentioning your cousin.'

"Oh yes. He is eighteen and very brilliant. In fact, he's one of those lucky guys who finds learning quite easy. When he was in junior high school, he was always at the top of his class; and, of course, he was expected to do the same when he went to senior high. What no one realized, and I still don't think his parents have quite realized, is that the high school he attended was a small school for local kids. Now that he's gone on to a university, the competition is tougher."

"And?"

"His grades are still quite high; but as the subjects get more intense, his scores are falling. His parents are worried and keep trying to force him to work harder—to the point that no matter what he achieves, it's not good enough."

"Give me an example, Chrissie."

"Well, if he gets a good test score, his father will say that he could have done better, instead of praising him for his accomplishment. Uncle is not unkind. I think that he wants to give Joss the impression that he can't ease up on his studies. A problem is developing. Joss is slipping further and further down the class ranks; and, of course, he's beginning to think of himself as a failure. He's under a lot of pressure from home and school because he really does have the ability."

As an afterthought, Chrissie added, "I think his parents would be more tolerant if Joss had siblings."

"You mean brothers or sisters?" I said, smiling to myself. Occasionally, we used different terminology for the same meaning. In the moment, I thought of the time when I asked Chrissie to come back and see me in a fortnight.

"In a WHAT!" she said with a completely blank look on her face.

"The American translation of fortnight is two weeks," I had explained.

"Well speak American...you're in America now," she had insisted.

For a second time, I realized that my concentration was wandering due to the absent healing. I was deep into my awareness of the other person, but, with some difficulty, I pulled myself back into the present. "Look, Chrissie, is there any chance of your coming back some other time, with your cousin? I'd like to discuss this problem with him."

"Would you see him tomorrow?"

"Of course, I'll be more logically aware tomorrow."

"Oh, that's great," she said. "Joss is staying with me at the moment, and this seems like an ideal opportunity. His parents think it's a good idea, too, so there are no difficulties with them."

The next day arrived quickly, and Chrissie and Joss came around for a late appointment. Chrissie amused herself by chatting with Debbie while Joss and I went to the treatment room. After a few minutes of general chat, as we became acquainted, Joss began to tell me about his problem.

"I feel like a failure already," he confided. "I know it's kind of stupid, but somehow I don't think I'm doing all this stuff for me. You know, getting a college degree and such."

"Who are you doing it for?"

"...the school, my tutor, my family. Obviously, I'm not making the grade. My folks have given me every means of support possible, but I'm just not getting this thing together."

"Do you know what your I.Q. is?"

"Yes, 167."

"That's high, Joss. Why do you think you're a failure?"

"...because I'm not getting the grades expected of me; and, if I am honest, I'm feeling like a failure because I know I could do better."

"What will you do when you eventually go out into the big world to earn a living?"

"...join the family business, I expect."

"What is that?"

"Oh, it's a big shipping business."

"Is that what you want to do?"

"I've never thought about it. Dad has always assumed I would. There's no one else in the family who could take it over. Grandfather started the business, and every one of the boys in the family have gone straight into it."

"But, Joss, do you want to?" I persisted.

"It's what's expected of me. Dad would be very hurt if I didn't. He says he's looking forward to the day when I take over."

"Ok, Joss," I said, "let's look at this from a different perspective. Imagine for a minute that there is no family business. Now, what are you going to do with your future?"

After a long silence, Joss looked at me, acting somewhat sheepishly and hesitatingly, and said, "I would like to own a flower shop."

"Have you told anyone else this?" I asked.

The fact that I hadn't looked shocked or made any comment about his response obviously gave Joss the confidence to continue. "Sure. I once, in a crazy moment, told my tutor that I would like to study horticulture and have my own flower shop."

"What did he say?"

"…went nuts…came completely unwrapped!"

"He what?"

"Sorry, my tutor came right back at me and said that I was being stupid—that I had a wonderful opportunity in my father's business. Worst of all, he said, and I know he's right, that having a flower shop would be a waste of a brain—a waste of my ability."

I didn't react, so Joss continued. "Then he really lost it. He told me how most of my friends would give anything to have my intellectual ability, my I.Q., or my opportunities. By the time he had finished, I felt as if I had been run over by a forty-ton truck!"

"I see," I said, looking directly into his eyes. "Joss, I want you to give me an honest answer to my next question."

"I'll try."

"Were you born to serve your I.Q., or is your I.Q. there to serve you?"

After thinking about my question for a moment, Joss brightened up. "Well, I'm sure as hell not going to work for my I.Q.," he said, beaming. "I seem to have enough masters already!"

"Good. So we agree. Whatever the level of your academic abilities, they are available to help you get what you want out of life—that you weren't born to serve your intellect. You don't have to have a job that equals your I.Q."

Joss nodded to express his agreement.

"What do you think would make your father proud of you, though I'm sure he already is?"

"Oh, yes, he is," Joss assured me. "We have great times together, and he does all he can to help, which is why I feel I'm letting him down so badly. I feel like a failure, because I think I'm disappointing him, after all he's done for me."

Joss was really beginning to open up now and was revealing what a pleasant, easy-going sort of man he was. He had natural ease about him and came across more artistic than scientific. "So think about it, Joss. What do you really believe your father wants for you?"

Again, Joss carefully thought through his reply before stating it. "It's what both my parents want...they want me to be happy, successful, and secure."

"Would your parents want you in the family business if you couldn't achieve those three aims?"

"No, Malcolm, I don't suppose they would. My father wouldn't want a sullen failure running his business."

"So, what must you do to achieve happiness, success, and security?" I asked him.

"...follow my own ambitions?"

"We are getting there, Joss."

"Will I be seen as a failure if I do follow my own ambitions ...by everyone?"

"You can only fail in life, Joss, if you allow others to set your standards. I'm not talking about moral responsibility and that sort of thing. In a civilized society, we must all accept certain standards of behavior. But regarding our abilities, our ambitions, and our self-worth, no one has the right to set these personal standards except ourselves."

I leaned forward and said, "Set your own goals, Joss. Decide what you want from life and use the wonderful abilities you have to achieve your aims. If at some future time you change your mind and decide to do something else, have the strength of character to change your life."

Joss was listening carefully, so I continued, "Provided you always know exactly what it is you want and you set your own standards for achievement, how can you possibly fail?"

Joss's beaming smile was all the encouragement I needed to make one more statement. "Failure is someone else's assessment of you, based on standards they set for themselves; and, incidentally, others usually see themselves as having failed and are living their dream through you."

"But what about my tutor?"

"Surely, Joss, if you know you are going to dictate your own aims and ambitions, you will be enthusiastic about your success. This is the way to satisfy everyone. Remember, enthusiasm is 99 percent of success."

Joss got up to leave. "You've certainly given me plenty to think about, and I agree with what you said about not letting my academic abilities dictate my future."

He hesitated before saying, "The strange thing is, I don't know that I really want the flower shop now that you've made it available. Instead, I can be anything I want to be. I feel a great sense of relief."

"Yes, Joss, that's right. Just remember, you are doing what you do for you. Your parents will be happy because you are happy. They have been trying in their own way to keep you going. Set your own standards by which you can achieve whatever it is you decide to do."

I said goodbye to Joss, closed the door, and waited for Chrissie to come in; but for the first time I could remember, she left without coming through to see me.

Chapter Fourteen
ABSENT HEALING

"Are you losing interest, Chrissie?"

"Why do you ask that?" she replied, looking quite hurt.

"Well, it's been almost a week since you were here with Joss. And, oh yes, you also forgot to say goodbye when you and Joss left."

"I thought you were being serious for a minute," she said with a laugh. "You know, I enjoy this verbal ping-pong between us."

"Who's keeping score, Chrissie? Am I losing?"

"I doubt it, Malcolm. You can just fly out of here and not even tell me, like you did last week. By the way, what was all that stuff about absent healing?"

"I probably spend more time in absent healing than I do in any other healing ways."

"What is absent healing, exactly?"

"Is this to be our subject for the day, Chrissie? It's a good one."

She adjusted her sitting position and settled in for another discussion. "A lot of people can't visit me in the office because they are too ill or too far away; and so I go to them instead, but not in a physical way. I think about them with loving thoughts, which they receive and use as if they were with me. This is true spiritual healing."

"Does a person need any special physical attributes to be able to do absent healing?" Chrissie asked.

"I've never really thought about it in a physical way," I replied, speaking honestly. "In fact, absent healing is not something I think about in any particular way—it's just a way of expressing Love. Because it does not require a physically active situation, people don't see it or become aware of it; and, therefore, I'm not often questioned about it."

"Well, Malcolm, I'm going to ask questions because I think, if I can grasp this, I will have a much better understanding of who you are and how you heal."

"What's the notebook for, Chrissie?" She hadn't taken notes of our discussions previously.

"I usually forget half of what you tell me, and you didn't seem to approve of the idea of using a tape recorder. So, I'm writing down the points that I think are important."

"I don't mind if you tape what I say, Chrissie. I was trying to make a point when you mentioned that you would like to record our discussions. I want you to find your own way to the truth; and if you get bogged down in my thoughts and experiences, and those of others, you may lose what I try to tell you. Listening to me is important, but you must start listening to your own inner voice, as well."

"Listen to my own inner voice? If I write that down, I shall be sure I made a mistake," she said, grinning. Then, with a burst of energy, Chrissie said: "Come on, Malcolm, let's get started or my time will pass before I've learned anything. I want to know how you heal."

"…the way I heal. Well, I don't need to have a lot of physical energy; but if a healer's energy is less than the client's, quite possibly, the healer will finish up taking energy from the client. Healing can be quite demanding."

Speaking with a serious tone, Chrissie asked, "Do you find healing demanding?"

"...not usually. I've learned how to make use of the client's own energy to release whatever emotional problems they have, and I also know how to replenish my reserves from energy that is readily available in the atmosphere."

"Is that why you're able to exist on such a small amount of food, Malcolm? I've never seen anyone eat as little as you do. Just one meal a day...and in the evening."

"Well, don't forget, Chrissie, I don't get involved in a lot of physical activity nowadays, so physically, I don't need much nourishment. I have no great need of energy to control emotions because I haven't allowed them to develop, and spiritual energy is infinite. So, I need only one meal a day to satisfy my physical needs."

"You just said that we need energy to control our emotions. I've never heard that before," Chrissie said, looking surprised.

"Oh, yes, fear has to be contained, and it takes a lot of energy to do that. It's possible to have so much fear that we use all of our energy trying to contain it. We then have insufficient energy left for normal activity. That's what causes the condition known as chronic fatigue syndrome. The emotion of fear is at a subconscious level, and not recognized by patient or doctor; but the only real answer to the problem is to bring the fear to the surface and deal with it logically. Then, the energy that has been containing the fear can be used for other purposes."

"Really?"

"Yes. One of the reasons people suffer stress is that they are trying to contain within themselves emotions of fear, greed, guilt, envy, and others in greater quantities than previous generations—because we are becoming an increasingly materialistic society. Of course, there are many reasons for stress, but all of the reasons usually come back to fear of some sort."

"So negative emotions are very damaging."

"Indeed, Chrissie. Some emotions, such as hate, anger, and jealousy, release energy to express the attitude; but if we try to contain the attitude, we use even more energy trying to suppress it. This brings the physical into conflict with itself and produces health-damaging symptoms such as heart attacks, multiple sclerosis, rheumatoid arthritis, and sciatica, to name a few. That's because the vibrations of fear are out of harmony with the body's natural rhythm. In some instances, fear has advantages; and in brief periods natural caution can save our lives. Today, however, many people are perpetually in fear. Anyway, we are getting off the subject."

"Sounds like us…back to absent healing."

"There are many ways of healing, Chrissie. When healing is conducted within a church, it's carried through in the form of prayers. All those taking part send prayers of loving support to the ones they want to help. This is a very effective way of healing."

"Do the prayers have to be said in a church, for them to work?" she asked.

"No. Not at all. Prayer groups working from their homes are just as effective. It's the sincerity and Love in the thoughts of those sending prayers that is all important, though having a picture in mind of the person or persons to be helped can make a huge difference. We talked about thinking with pictures a few weeks ago, didn't we?"

I could tell that Chrissie was in deep thought as she answered by saying, "Yes, I remember the importance of communicating with pictures." Then, her next question came out quickly. "Can anyone say prayers to help other people?" she asked.

Chrissie was sensing that this was something she could become involved in. "Absolutely," I replied. You don't have to belong to any organized religion in order to send loving thoughts, as prayers, to help others. Unfortunately, thoughts of superiority have caused some to claim that only their form of belief has any credibility with God. Those who believe this way find fault with all other thoughts of Love in order to make their own seem superior, but we discussed this earlier, as well."

"So, Malcolm, do you use prayers to heal?"

"Every thought is a prayer, Chrissie. Good or bad, every thought is a prayer. Thinking is praying, though few people look at it that way. Going to church and having lovely caring thoughts for a few hours one day a week is no good if for the rest of the week your thinking is in opposition to your thoughts on the day or in the hours you pray. The thoughts you live by affect your life, and the lives of those around you, not what you think while in prayer."

"I understand," she said, "but you talked about leaving your body during absent healing."

"The more one becomes total Love, Chrissie, the less emotion hangs about the bodily spirit. This state makes it increasingly easy to move as Love from the physical body."

"A lot of people will dislike hearing this," she said, sounding and looking worried.

"Why do you say that?" I asked.

"Well, many people, whether spiritual healers or not, can't leave their bodies and will feel slighted or hurt in some way."

"Oh, you mean their egos will have difficulty. That's ok, Chrissie. Spiritual healers have been putting up with little difficulties like these for hundreds of years. Many religions haven't been able to handle the thought of someone being able to do what they couldn't."

"I guess that's why some people threw stones and hurt people who could," Chrissie reasoned.

"That's right, and it still happens, of course. But in this century, science and logic have suffered from a surfeit of egotism."

"A what? What's a surfeit?"

"An excess...too much."

"Oh, I see, and agree."

Chrissie was really with me on this subject and was carrying the topic along rather than prodding it, which was her usual way. "Logical, scientific minds have been having fun for years with people who have greater vision or insight, but who lack the intellectual ability to explain themselves," she said.

"You're right. However, a great change is happening, and people are becoming more spiritually aware and beginning to re-evaluate their goals and reasons for what they are trying to achieve. More and more people are freeing themselves of whatever stands in the way of becoming one with Love and the strength and knowledge found with Love."

"Ok, Malcolm, let's get back to absent healing! You were talking about leaving the body. How do you explain that?"

"Chrissie, my voice is all over this room, in front of me, behind me, and everywhere in the room. Just because it has left my lips doesn't mean it's not me, ok?"

"Yes," she agreed, "I can see that. Your thoughts caused the sound, so it's part of you."

"And my thoughts, which made the sound, travel out into all time and space. There's no place my thoughts cannot reach. Are you still with me?"

Chrissie confirmed that she was and said she had no difficulty understanding that the energy of a thought was not limited by time or space. "Once I'm free of my body, and free of emotion, there's no place my thoughts cannot be. They exist as Love energy in every sphere. All that's needed is to direct the force of the Love, which is the spirit, to where it's needed or being requested."

"Wow! So you're telling me that you can be any place where you direct your thoughts…think yourself to, right?"

"Yes, Chrissie. Why should I ever think that I'm restricted by time or body to *a place*. As total Love, we can become one with anything or anyone who requests Love. It's not a matter of going here or there—Love is already there. Love has no need of identification, or personality. Why limit yourself to a place when, as Love, you can be one with all that is."

"Awesome! This concept is difficult to grasp, but it's awesome."

I asked Chrissie to close her eyes; and soon, she was lost in a sea of sensations, as she floated into a non-physical place. In that instant, Chrissie lost her understanding of identity, and the Love that she was drew her up into itself. Instead of Love coming from Chrissie, Chrissie became the Love. In this totally relaxed state, she exuded a great sense of peace and calm.

"What are you aware of, Chrissie?"

"A bright light," she told me. "I seem to be surrounded by this unbelievably beautiful bright light."

"Let it wash over you and through you, Chrissie. Feel it dissolving any negative emotions, until you become one with the Light."

After a few minutes in a state of total peace and contentment, Chrissie quietly told me that she had become one with the Light. I continued to guide her by saying, "Think of someone, Chrissie, who is in need of Love and help; and when you have a picture of them in your thoughts, travel as that thought to the person who needs your Love. Tell me when you reach them."

After a few more seconds, Chrissie told me she was with a friend. She could see the person in her mind.

"Let the Love, the Light which you've become, shine on the person you've gone to and give yourself totally to the degree that they will accept the Love you are. See the Light you've become and fold it around your friend, so they will become one with the Light also."

Chrissie assured me that she was sharing Love and Light with her friend, so I asked her to think of another needy friend, or a relative or an animal, whom she felt Love for. "And now, Chrissie," I suggested, "go to the second person as Love and Light and do exactly the same. This time, keep the first person in your thoughts, your Love, as you move to the next. Now, you are with both of them at the same time."

Shortly, she quietly told me she was with the second person and that the first friend was still in her Light. I let her remain in that state for a few minutes and then asked her to repeat the procedure, keeping the first two in her Love and Light while bringing a third into her thoughts. Within a minute, Chrissie whispered to me that she had all three people in her Light.

She stayed in the euphoric state for about fifteen minutes and then, I asked her to release the three people from her thoughts and to return to the center of the Light she had started from. From there, I asked her to return to her physical shell. A few minutes passed before Chrissie opened her eyes—and even longer before she spoke. She had a beautiful, radiant glow all over her, around her, and through her. I waited for Chrissie to speak first.

"That was so beautiful," was all she could say. She was full of Love, and the joy and contentment that is part of it.

"You just returned from your first journey into absent healing."

"But I didn't say any prayers, or anything," she said, as if she had forgotten something.

"Why would you have to say prayers?" I asked, smiling. "The Love and Light you are said everything. Chrissie, you were the prayer. Don't you see, this is what I've been teaching you right from the beginning…Love is who you *are*. A prayer is what you *are*, not what you *do*. The Love and tenderness that caused you to give of yourself for others in need makes praying unnecessary. To pray would have separated you from the Light. You were the Light! You *are* Love; and when you live that way, you become a living, breathing prayer of Love. The Love, the Light, comes from God. You were directing the Love you *are* to those who needed it."

Knowing that some other people might not be ready to agree with my beliefs about Love and Light, I tried to caution Chrissie by saying, "Some, of course, will say that this is the work of the devil, and…"

"That's impossible!" she said, interrupting. "God's Love was everywhere. I could touch it, hear it, feel it, and see it. The only devil would be in denying Love."

"I know, Chrissie, but don't be disappointed if people don't understand when you try to explain the beauty of healing Love.

Don't forget what I've told you—many of those who can't achieve higher standards will find fault with those who can, in order to maintain their own ego."

"This might frighten some people, too, Malcolm."

"I agree. Fear is a strong emotion, and the shades I told you about will do all they can to keep others in the dark, in the emotions of fear, possessiveness, and superiority. Unfortunately, this includes some religious types."

Chrissie was still overcome by the beauty of her experience. "Am I a healer now?" she asked.

"If you have Love in your heart, how could you be anything else?"

"I know," she said, starting with a laugh. "Love is who you *are*. Now, I really understand what you mean by Love. Is there any limit to the number of people who can be helped with Love, Malcolm? I mean, I know, and now understand, what you mean by being in more than one place at the same time. So why don't you, and others, use absent healing to heal everyone?"

"Now you are changing the subject, Chrissie."

"How am I doing that?" she asked, looking surprised.

"You're getting back to asking me to *do* something. I don't *do* anything with Love, Chrissie. You didn't *do* anything when you were with your friends in the Light. You were just there as Love, for your friends to make use of if they wanted to. Love is available for everyone, irrespective of race, religious beliefs, or anything else you care to mention; and everyone has it within them. To release Love, all people need to do is move away from fear and other negative emotions."

Looking perplexed, Chrissie asked, "So what's the problem?"

"There is no problem, but people must ask for help. We can't just go around taking people into healing Love because we feel good about it. Healers wouldn't withhold Love from anyone, but people must usually ask, through prayer or word, to receive it. If people pray for help, it becomes available to them as Love."

Still looking perplexed, her next question was: "But, Malcolm what about healing?"

"You see, Chrissie, healing is not important—it's not what my work is all about. Healing is only a way of making people aware that Love is their natural spiritual state. All other emotional states those brought on through fear, possessiveness, or superiority, are unnatural. That's why people suffer so much."

Chrissie was annoyed that I wasn't willing to rush about and heal everyone, and she couldn't wait to ask, "If healing is not important, why do you do it?"

"I heal because people ask me to," I replied, "but if people stop asking, I will enjoy doing something else. If I heal without being asked, I assume authority over other people's needs. That's the emotion of superiority or ego."

"Oh," was her only response.

"It's not our personality or emotions that are special," I continued. "It's the Love we *are*, which we cannot know of, that's so special. Because we cannot know of our own Love, Chrissie, we bask in the radiance and beauty of Love radiated to us through others."

"I just wish I could really understand how Love originates " Chrissie said sincerely.

"All Love has one source, The Greatest of All Love, recognized in the name of God. I'm referring to the Love that we all see in others. This Love is always available. At times, however, we allow emotion to block its brightness; or even worse, we obliterate it when we ignore Love and become some negative emotion, like hate."

"Well, I know that I've experienced Love, Malcolm, and perhaps that's enough for now."

"Perhaps, Chrissie. You see, God speaks to us through the beauty He has placed in the life around us, and we speak to Him with the Love we pass on to others."

Chapter Fifteen
SPIRITUAL HEALING

"Hello Chrissie! ...lovely day. I thought you would have preferred to be outside enjoying the beauty of the flowers, the trees, the birds, and the sun, rather than sitting in here."

"Ok, then let's go outside," she suggested. "We don't have to stay in here."

"...good idea; let's do it. I'll just tell Debbie we're on the terrace, if she needs me."

Soon, we were outside and sitting under the shade of a ficus tree. "The problem with sitting outside, Chrissie, is that the environment is hypnotic. Listen to the birds singing their beautiful songs and the Katydids humming the chorus lines. I love the feel of the breeze as it sways the trees in harmony with the melody. The choreography of nature's performance is amazing."

"Yes, isn't it. The warm air is relaxing, and I may have difficulty concentrating. Keep the topic light, Malcolm."

"...depends on your questions, Chrissie."

"Alright, can you tell me what happened last week? That was really cool. One minute, I was listening, totally absorbed, to your explanation of absent healing; the next, I was entering a beautiful white light. I'm still basking in the beauty and pure magic of it."

"Have your thoughts and emotions been different since your last visit?" I asked.

"Oh yes, I've been calmer and quieter...more so than I can ever remember. I've had a sense of peace within me that I can't explain. Right after I left your office, I was on a high—it was great; I was so energized I thought I would fly. The exhilaration was wonderful. This sensation lasted about two days; and then, I started to relax and feel wonderfully calm and content inside. My anxiety and stress have left me...everything seems more peaceful now."

"Everything? Or just you, Chrissie?"

She thought for a moment. "No, I suppose my reactions and attitudes have changed. And sleep...wow! I'm getting a full night's sleep now. I used to dream a lot—be restless through the night; but my nights are peaceful now. I'm not remembering any dreams."

"What else?"

"Well, I'm seeing things differently, too. I feel part of everything—not separate. This feeling seems weird at times."

"What do you mean by weird, Chrissie?"

"Before last week, I used to concentrate on whatever I wanted to create—studied it first, looked at it in depth, and put a lot of thought into it. I'm not doing any of that now—everything just works out. I just don't put as much thought into my art. This is difficult to explain...somehow I'm in the painting when I'm working. The best way I can describe it is to say that I'm painting with my mind, not my brush."

She thought about her own comments for a moment before asking, "What happened to change my perceptions, Malcolm? What did you do?"

"I didn't *do* anything, Chrissie, as I've explained many times."

"Is that what you call healing? I didn't feel ill or anything; but, somehow, I feel I've improved physically and mentally since last week."

"That's a perfect example of spiritual healing, Chrissie."

"It is?"

"Of course it is. Healing people of this or that is not so important. True spiritual healing is creating a situation with Love, which allows people to become themselves. It doesn't always happen after the first healing, though it can, depending on the amount of emotion that has to be removed and whether the client is truly prepared to let go of the excuses they've been using as reasons for the attitudes they've become."

"I feel you've released me from something, Malcolm, so I'm free to be alive. Is that because you removed my fears?"

"Yes, that's part of it, but only the preparation. The change, as you put it, came when you gave of yourself to help others. When you stopped thinking of Chrissie and saw the beauty in the life around you, being a creative artist became easier for you. You deal with nature in your art, so you are already in tune with spirit."

"Did the change in me happen, Malcolm, when I became the Light and let whatever the Light was be taken by people who needed it? Are you telling me that the absent healing was healing me? If it was, I hadn't expected to be healed."

"…something like that, Chrissie. I'll try to explain. This part is a bit difficult to put across, so be patient."

She smiled and nodded. "Spiritual healing is all about unconditional and absolute Love. Unconditional means to totally accept the person who asks for help without any pre-conditions. I mean total acceptance with no conditions! For example, how could you successfully give healing to a person who'd had an abortion if you believed that what they did was wrong?"

"How could I not think about it?"

"If you think about whether a person is right or wrong, you immediately put a condition into your Love. Let's try another example—something less obvious than a moral issue. Something as innocent as thinking 'I wish these people didn't smoke' or 'She is five minutes late' places conditions on your Love. The Love you are immediately becomes conditional when judgments of any kind go through your mind. By having negative thoughts or judgments, emotion is introduced into the healing thoughts, which begins to block the flow of Love to those you want to help, and to yourself as well."

"Becoming unconditional Love isn't easy, is it, Malcolm?"

"It all comes down to being able to totally accept, in every way, anyone who asks for help…including everyone…no exceptions, even people who probably don't totally accept you. If the healing Love you are offering is going to be spiritual and fully effective, there can be no exceptions. The reverse is also true. Only when the healer is accepted unconditionally will those who ask for help be able to receive all the help or Love being offered."

"I thought we were keeping this discussion light," Chrissie chided.

"Look for the simplicity, Chrissie. Spiritual Love accepts everyone as equals without any conditions and makes itself available to all life forms whenever it is requested. Conditions are formed by emotions that act as blocks to healing—to receiving healing as well as giving healing."

"Well, Malcolm, I can't say that I would find it easy to accept everyone as totally as you're suggesting. Does this mean that I won't be able to receive healing or to become a healer?"

"No, Chrissie." Her sincerity caused me to give her a reassuring smile. "But you will be limiting your ability to heal to the degree that you find yourself liking or disliking, approving or disapproving, accepting or not accepting the Love and life around you, particularly those who come to you for help. As I've said before, you limit the abilities of your own body to heal itself or protect itself by the attitudes you have towards others."

"Tell me, Malcolm, what goes through your mind when someone walks through your doorway?" Chrissie asked. She was obviously puzzled by the spiritual requirements of Love.

"That's an easy question to answer, Chrissie. First, I look for the beauty and Love that I see in all life; and then, I become one with it, just like you did when you became the white light. By harmonizing with other people's Love, anything not of Love is separated out. That's all. Chrissie, it never crosses my mind that I should do anything for anyone."

"Surely, Malcolm, you must want to do something to help?"

"Oh, Chrissie, we've been here before. I don't *do* anything. I can't *do* anything with the Love I am. I don't even know of the Love I am. Did you *do* anything with the white light, when you were absent healing?"

Her head moved from side to side immediately. "Of course not," I continued, "your friends did something with it. You added to their Love, which made it possible for their spirits to rise above any negative emotions. That way, the negative emotions become separated, and the Love inside can dissolve or change them. The body then returns to its normal healthy state."

Chrissie's blank look prompted me to have another go at this explanation. "I'll try to explain it another way," I began. "Imagine that a little girl with cerebral palsy and all the difficulties associated with that condition has just been brought into my treatment room. The thought that I could alter her, change her, or improve her in some way would never cross my mind."

"Why is that?" Chrissie asked, as she moved her chair to escape the direct rays of the sun, which had come from behind the shelter of the tree.

"Because I Love children, all children, just as they are, Chrissie. To me, they are absolutely perfect—whatever their condition may be. They are already a radiant white light of Love. Why on Earth would I want to change them? For such a thought to enter my mind, even for a second, is unthinkable. All children are perfect as they are; all are beautiful. All children are wrapped in Love, even those who struggle more than others to be accepted. I want them to see their own light, their own beauty. If I see it, I can reflect it back to them; and they will be able to accept themselves. They will feel the Love they are and cause their own change or improvement."

"You're amazing, Malcolm."

"No, Chrissie, I'm not amazing. I just know that if for a moment I begin to think that children can be changed or helped, if I think I can improve their conditions, I have judged them as being less than perfect. How can any child of Love be less than perfect?"

"It's impossible, if we withhold judgments, isn't it, Malcolm?"

"Yes. If I should decide that I can improve their little lives by changing their physical state in some way, I would have to create a vision in my mind as to how I am going to improve their lives. I would need to see them differently from their present condition. In other words, I would not accept them as they are."

"Could a child feel your thoughts?"

"Immediately, Chrissie. At a deeper subconscious or spiritual level, children will sense that they have not been accepted as they are, that they have been judged inferior in some way; and they will immediately put up an emotional barrier of resistance, trying to keep my emotions of imperfections out of their thoughts."

While moving her chair again to avoid the sun, Chrissie asked, "Why would children create such strong emotional barriers?"

"Because they will feel my rejection of them as they are. We can't reject this bit and accept that bit. We either accept and Love someone totally, unconditionally, or reject them. Children know who Loves them and who accepts them as they are. In my work, I have seen the most beautiful Love for children coming from parents and grandparents."

"Oh, Malcolm, you can't be saying that parents who try to help their children may reject them on some level. That's a terrible thought."

"No, I don't mean that sort of help. That's the beautiful Love I spoke of when I mentioned parents who totally accept and Love their children, and do all they can to ensure the child has every opportunity that life can offer for the improvement of their lives. Parental Love is the strongest Love of all; and to help the child, we must also accept and Love the parent. I can't heal a child if I reject the person the child Loves, parent or not."

"Slow down, Malcolm! You're in overdrive again."

"Alright, Chrissie. You see, when you can accept someone for who they are, without conditions or judgments, they can then accept your Love and use it to change themselves, if they choose.

Healing Love dissolves hurt and fear, builds confidence and self-respect, and allows the one being healed to change their own condition to the extent that is physically possible."

I wanted to be sure that Chrissie was understanding. "Can't you see how beautiful it all is?" I asked. "Spiritual healing is not about doing anything—it's about seeing beauty and Love in others. There can be no responsibility or purpose in that kind of Love. I'm talking about total acceptance of another into your home, your life. It goes back to what I told you several weeks ago. We have no purpose. Others make us their purpose and use the Love we are to change themselves, provided we don't put conditions on our Love."

Chrissie was squirming. "Is the sun bothering you?" I asked.

"Yes, it is, just a bit; but I didn't want to interrupt."

"Ok, let's go back inside."

"Wow, Malcolm, it's cold in here, after being in the sun."

"Some people are never satisfied," I said, digging at Chrissie.

Her look was chilling, too. "Can I go over the main points of this spiritual healing thing? Sorry…I mean Love." Chrissie had her notebook out. "If I'm right," she continued, "all you have to do to be a spiritual healer is totally accept whoever comes to you for help, without any thoughts of *doing* anything for them."

"Yes, that's right; but don't forget, to be able to heal that way, you need to be free of negative emotion yourself and allow the Love that is your natural state to take over."

"Come on, Malcolm. I've seen you healing, and you *do* more than talk. You stand behind people and place your hands over them. Surely, you're *doing* something."

"Yes, Chrissie, but that's not strictly spiritual healing. What you described is magnetic or energy healing, and it's sometimes necessary to bring people to a meditative state, which helps them to separate from the emotion that is causing their problems."

"Aren't we discussing spiritual healing?"

"Yes, but the energy that flows through my hands is not Love, Chrissie. It's a physical energy that I use to help people move more quickly into the meditation state by slowing mind activity. By moving people into the meditative state, I can help them release the emotions that are causing them problems. That's possible because the physical energies will have been brought into harmony with spiritual Love."

"...sounds very complicated," Chrissie said, sighing.

"No, it isn't, really. Using physical energy is just a matter of knowing where to put your hands to create the required healing state and to move physical energy into harmonizing patterns."

"And what is the state a spiritual healer helps a client reach?"

"One of Love...freedom from subconscious fears and negative thoughts."

Chrissie's body language told me that she wasn't going to continue this discussion much longer, which was a relief. I wasn't sure whether I was repeating myself. "You are firm in your belief that you don't *do* anything, aren't you?"

"Emphatically! Love is who we *are*, Chrissie. We are all part of spiritual Love, if we choose to be and rid ourselves of negative or selfish emotions."

Realizing the time, I said, "I need to make a few phone calls, Chrissie. Can we call it a day?"

"Sure," she replied. "I'll go and have some coffee with Debbie—and make an appointment for next week."

Debbie brought me a glass of iced tea when I finished my calls. She grinned and said: "You've got one very excited lady out there. She has some news and would like to see you again, just for a few minutes."

Chrissie came in immediately and sat down. I could see the glow of joy that was radiating from her. "Hope you don't mind," she started, "but Debbie said it would be ok. In fact, she suggested it."

"Suggested what?" I was almost as impatient as Chrissie could be. Her excitement was infectious.

"I was telling Debbie about the absent healing I did with you last week, and she suggested that I phone the people I visited as healing light to check on them. "It's just too incredible to be true." Chrissie's excitement was barely confinable.

"Chrissie, just tell me the news."

"Oh, Malcolm, the first friend I phoned has had 'baby blues' for two years since she gave birth to her second child. When I called her, she told me that during the afternoon about a week ago she suddenly began to feel more like she was before the baby was born."

By now, Chrissie's excitement had reached fever pitch; and I must admit that I felt excitement for her, as I recalled the first time someone told me how much better they felt after I sent absent healing. "And the second call?"

"Almost the same," she said. "…except the other friend I went to is actually an aunt who's been told that she has a shadow on her lung. As you can understand, she's been terribly worried. I know she won't be aware of any change in her condition, even if there has been improvement. We have always been close, and she's only in her fifties. So, wouldn't it be nice to think that I helped in some way?"

"Well, of course." I was getting as bad as Chrissie. Her excitement was catching.

"She just told me that she knew somehow that I was with her last week. She didn't know why or how, but she just knew. Since then, all of her worries and anxieties have lifted. She said she just knows that everything is going to be alright, and she has had the best week she's had in a long time."

"Chrissie, that's wonderful! So now you know…everyone can heal. All it takes is to remove all doubt and negative emotion from your mind and to enter into unconditional Love.

Chapter Sixteen
ANGER

"Hi, Malcolm. I'd like you to meet my friend, Jenny."

Jenny was slim, about thirty-three, unmarried, and obviously very nervous. I couldn't help thinking it was only Chrissie's strong personality that had persuaded Jenny to enter the building at all. They seated themselves in opposite chairs, and Jenny looked nervously across at Chrissie.

"I asked Jenny to come with me," Chrissie began, "because I think you might be able to help her. She's had multiple sclerosis for several years; and although hers is not very debilitating, it's slowly getting worse. I'm sure you can help, right?"

I turned my attention to Jenny. "You're not sure about this healing stuff, are you?" I asked, giving her a smile.

"No, not really."

"Well, don't worry about it, Jenny. I'm really quite harmless; and, anyway, all you need do is to tell me about your symptoms. I'll try to explain how healing can help."

"Really, there isn't a lot I can tell you," Jenny replied, settling back in her chair, which was half way between being to the front and side of me.

"Then just tell me what you can."

"I first noticed that I was becoming weaker in my left side

when I was about twenty. I thought nothing about it at first; but as my leg continued to become increasingly weaker, I went to have some tests. The doctor's diagnosis was multiple sclerosis."

"What sort of work do you do, Jenny?"

"I'm a secretary with an insurance company."

"Do you have any phobias?"

Jenny thought for a moment before answering, "Not that I'm aware of."

"Any recurring dreams?"

"No."

Jenny began to relax and told me more about herself. Nothing in particular was extraordinary about her life. She did not have any boyfriends, had never been married, and had lived alone in a big city since she was twenty-five. Now, it was Jenny's turn to question me.

"What, exactly, do you do?" she asked.

"Not a lot really, especially with a condition like your own. Experience has taught me that multiple sclerosis is a very physical condition; however, it's cause, which is what we are more interested in, is usually emotional."

I had already noticed that Jenny was a very sensitive soul, which is not unusual for people with this condition. Multiple sclerosis sufferers are often the most loving, tender, and gentle people you could ever meet. Jenny was no exception. The healing Love was beginning to have its effect, and Jenny was already showing signs of becoming emotional.

"The doctors have given me very definite physical reasons for my symptoms," she volunteered. "They tell me that my leg is weak because the myelin sheath that protects the nerves in the spine are breaking down."

"Yes, Jenny, but those are just symptoms of a deeper cause."

"But the doctors say that the cause of my weakness is multiple sclerosis."

"That's just a fancy Latin name for a particular set of symptoms," I countered, smiling, "which tell us very little. What we are interested in is why your body is not protecting you against these symptoms."

"How do you mean?" she asked.

"Well, people with multiple sclerosis are usually beautiful, kind, generous, patient, and often sensitive people, like yourself; but underneath, they are angry—sometimes seething about some injustice, which they think they suffered earlier in their lives or perhaps are still tolerating. I suspect that in spite of your lovely, quiet nature you are in fact very, very angry about something; and you either don't know how to let it go or you haven't the means to do so."

Jenny went quiet for a while. Her pursed lips indicated that she was struggling with some emotion, as the healing Love began to bring it to the surface. "I think I know what I'm probably angry about," she said, speaking so quietly that her voice was barely audible.

I was hoping that Chrissie would have the good sense to remain quiet. I glanced her way and noticed that she had reclined deeper into her chair, being as unobtrusive as possible. Jenny, having moved into the healing Love, had become unaware of Chrissie's presence.

"Tell me about it, Jenny."

"Well, I don't want to make a fuss about nothing," she started. "Lots of people have to put up with far worse than anything that's happened to me."

"Tell me about it, anyway."

"There's not much to tell, really. When I was little, about six years old, my little sister was born. She was never very strong and died of a heart condition when she was six. But from the day she was born, everyone seemed to forget me. See, Malcolm, I told you it was silly, didn't I?"

"Did you feel angry towards your little sister?"

"Oh, no. We loved each other; and after she died, I felt terribly lonely."

"Who were you angry with, or rather, who are you angry with?"

"Grandpa."

"Why?"

"Because up until my little sister was born, we used to spend lots of time together—going for walks, shopping, and all those sorts of things. After the baby was born, he spent all of his time looking after her. He didn't even seem to notice I was there. Sometimes, he would take my toys for my little sister to play with, even when I was still playing with them."

Jenny was really beginning to unwind. Tears rolled down her cheeks as she continued to tell me how her love for Grandpa went unnoticed.

"But I think that perhaps the worst of all," she continued, "was after she died. I was on my own again and thought Grandpa and I would do things together, like before, but it didn't happen that way. Whenever I wanted to go for a walk, and tried to put my hand in his, he would turn away and say, 'Not now, Jenny.' No one would talk about her, and this made it all worse, as if she'd never been there. Grandpa was more despondent than anyone. He turned away from us after she died."

I handed the tissue box to Jenny. She still had tears to release. "I know I'm being silly, Malcolm, because I know now that Grandpa was sad and lonely and that he missed my little sister terribly. Mom said to leave him alone—that I reminded him of her, which made it all seem worse. I suppose I was just being selfish."

"Is Grandpa still alive?"

"No, he died about ten years ago. He never got over my sister's death; and after she died, he totally ignored me. Please don't think I'm complaining about my little sister. It wasn't her fault, and I missed her, too. I just have this nasty jealousy thing in my head, which makes me angry when I think about my Grandpa. It really wasn't anything to complain about. Mom and Dad have always loved me, but I wanted Grandpa's love and attention."

"I want you to do something for me, Jenny."

"Yes, what's that?"

"I want you to close your eyes."

Jenny obediently closed her tear-strained eyes, as if she was relieved to avoid the present. "I want you to see yourself as the little girl you once were," I instructed. "I want you to take your thoughts back to the time when you were feeling at your loneliest—to the time you felt most rejected and unhappy. Can you see yourself as you were then?"

"Yes," Jenny whispered, tears streaming.

"Now, Jenny, take that little girl in your arms and give her a big cuddle. Feel little Jenny and put her arms around your neck. Feel your love flowing into her…feel little Jenny's love flowing into you. Are you able to do this?"

"I'm not sure," Jenny responded, still weeping.

"But why, Jenny? That little girl needs your love."

"Because she's not very nice, is she?"

"How could a little girl of six or seven not be very nice, Jenny, all she wants is to be loved. She's been rejected by her Grandpa. Are you going to reject her, as well?"

At this point, Jenny totally broke down in great heaving sobs. "Come on, Jenny," I continued. "If a little girl came through the door right now, feeling lonely, rejected, and unloved, would you tell her that she wasn't very nice? Would you tell her to stop crying, to pull herself together, to snap out of it, or to stop being silly? Would you say that it's no great deal to be turned away by Grandpa? Or, would you take her in your arms and give her a big, big love?"

Sobbing, Jenny said, "I would take her in my arms and love her."

"Then why can't you love the little girl who was you?"

I hesitated, as Jenny reacted to my question. She seemed hesitant. "Come on, Jenny, that little girl deserves your love. She wants your love more than any other love in the world. Wrap your arms around her. Can you do that now?"

"Yes," she said. "I'm holding her." With her eyes still closed and weeping, she quietly rocked herself to and fro.

I glanced at Chrissie; she was weeping quietly.

"You know, Jenny," I continued, "that little girl never did anything bad. All she wanted was to be loved by you and Grandpa."

"I know," she cried, "but Grandpa used to tell me to stop sulking or that I was being jealous, when I was quiet or feeling unhappy. I know my sister needed lots of attention and love because she was sick, but he didn't have to totally ignore me, did he?"

"No, Jenny, he shouldn't have ignored you. Little Jenny also needed a lot of love. You were unhappy and lonely; and, because Grandpa told you that you were being naughty when you felt rejected, you blamed yourself."

She nodded.

"You couldn't blame your little sister because you knew it wasn't her fault. You couldn't blame Grandpa because you loved him. Anyway, hadn't he told you it was your fault? Be sure to tell the little Jenny how much you love her, Jenny. Tell her how pretty she is…that she never was a bad girl."

Jenny was calmer now and said, "I know, Malcolm. If only he had loved me after my sister died…he didn't seem to love anyone after that; and he never held me again."

"Continue to feel little Jenny's love pour into you and your love flow into her. She's a beautiful little girl, and the only love in the world she needs is yours. How can anyone else love her, Jenny, if you don't. If you don't think she is worthy of love, neither will anyone else."

We sat quietly for moment before I said, "Now, Jenny, I want you to do something else for me."

"What's that?" she asked. Her eyes were still closed.

"I want you to see Grandpa. Can you do that?"

She replied with a slow, hesitant, "Yes."

"You see, Jenny, Grandpa didn't understand. He still loved you—he just didn't understand how to cope with the situation. It wasn't his fault. He was very worried about your little sister. We can't know what was going through his mind. Can you still see Grandpa in your mind?"

"Yes."

"What do you think Grandpa would do, Jenny, if he could sit here with us and listen to all of this, if you were to tell him you forgive him...that you still love him very, very much."

Jenny was silent for a moment. Then she said, "I think he would cry. I think he would take me in his arms and just say 'I didn't know. I'm sorry.'"

"So, Jenny, see Grandpa in your mind and take him in your arms. Give him a big cuddle and a big love. Feel his love for you."

At this, Jenny released all her emotion.

"Let all the anger you've been feeling for years, Jenny, go back to Grandpa. I want you to let all the love you feel for Grandpa come to the surface. Can you feel the love instead of the anger?"

"I can, Malcolm. I can feel him taking all my anger; I can feel his love for me."

"You see, Jenny, while you were holding the anger inside you, there was nothing Grandpa could do to put it right. He needs to be able to take the anger he caused back to himself so he can feel the pain he caused and change it. He's replacing the anger with love."

"I know. I can feel it," Jenny said, letting go with a big, deep sigh.

After letting Jenny hold Grandpa in her thoughts for a few minutes, I asked her to return her thoughts to little Jenny and to hold her once more. "I want you to tell little Jenny that you will never leave her again."

"Oh, I won't!"

"...and if ever you feel sad, lonely, or rejected, you will go into a quiet place, take little Jenny in your arms, and give her a cuddle. You see, Jenny, she lost her self-respect and confidence, but she has it back now. If you feel angry or impatient again, I want you to see Grandpa and just give him a big love. Little Jenny has had the problem, Jenny, not you; but she will be alright now."

After a little while, Jenny opened her eyes and gave me a beautiful smile. "I feel wonderful!" she said. "Somehow, I'm calmer and more peaceful inside. I know I've been healed."

"You will overcome the multiple sclerosis now, Jenny. The anger and unhappiness have gone, and your body can heal itself."

Chrissie gave Jenny a big hug as they both floated out of the room.

Chapter Seventeen
REJECTION

"Hi, Chrissie!" She had called and asked to see us on her way to an appointment. "I thought you were organizing some sort of picnic for our next meeting. Got it sorted yet?"

"I would have, but I have a friend who can never manage the dates I suggest; and whenever I ask her to share her own ideas, she comes up with impossible alternatives."

"Sounds as if you've got a rejection type there," Debbie commented.

"How's that, Debbie?" I asked. "I don't think she's being rejected or rejecting the idea of a picnic."

"Oh, you can just tell, Malcolm. Those types always want the times you've already said aren't available, and they can never make it at a time that suits others."

Chrissie turned to me and asked, "Is that right?"

"Yes, rejection types, using Debbie's terms, are usually people who suffered some great rejection when they were little and now live in fear of being rejected again. As if to prove themselves right, they go out of their way to be rejected."

"But that's a crazy way to behave!" Chrissie said emphatically.

"Maybe it is, Chrissie, but people with rejection personalities aren't aware of what they're doing."

"So what do we do about her, Malcolm?"

"Just be firm and make sure your friend has a place in the arrangements; she'll turn up."

"Ok, I'll plan the picnic for next Sunday afternoon. See you both there."

Come Sunday afternoon, about twelve people gathered for Chrissie's party, which was more like a royal feast than a picnic. I'd never seen so much food for so few people! The setting was idyllic—on the side of a river in a field of green grass. A group of tree stumps was quite useful as chairs for those of us who felt the ground was a little out of reach.

"Is the friend who had such difficulty organizing her time the girl who's doing all the work?" I asked Chrissie. "…the one in the green and white dress?"

"You mean Kate. Yes, how did you know?"

"Because she's so busy looking after people and entertaining everyone."

"Oh, she's always like that, Malcolm. She's full of fun; and if you want a job done, ask Kate to do it. That's why I was so surprised when you suggested that she was probably looking for rejection. Nobody could possibly reject Kate—she's such fun and always the best at a party."

"That's one of her traits, Chrissie. People with personalities like Kate's are driven by fear of rejection and are always subconsciously looking for it. If you do something for them, they will exaggerate what you've done. You know what I mean—go over the top."

"You've just described Kate, exactly. She's a very likable girl, and she overwhelms the people she likes with love and praises. In fact, it can be a bit embarrassing because she's sometimes really excessive in her generosity."

"That's when she's pushing someone to reject her. Be careful when you observe this behavior. If she ever believes you have rejected her, she will fly into a rage. She will become a most unforgiving person."

"You've just explained a lot, Malcolm. A mutual friend didn't invite her to a party last year because she thought Kate was being a bit pushy. Wow! Kate's reaction nearly split our group. Her attitude was very destructive—not at all like the Kate we knew. Why would she behave like that?"

"As I told you, people who are driven by a fear of rejection usually create a situation that will eventually cause rejection. Then, they release their anger and resentment, which has been building in their subconscious for years. These people are a bit like a volcano, always looking for an opportunity to explode. Be sure you're not in the way when it happens."

"By the way, Malcolm, thanks for what you did for Jenny last week."

"Jenny's case was just a matter of replacing unhappiness and anger with Love."

"Jenny's problem was rejection, but she's nothing like Kate. Is she?"

"Jenny can accept herself now. So, she'll become more confident and start meeting people. She no longer has a reason to believe that other people dislike her; she has learned how to like herself. Self-rejection is one of the hardest things to live with, Chrissie. It's always there. Other people feel or sense it and tend to avoid anyone lacking confidence, which just confirms the belief of worthlessness in the thoughts of the rejected."

"I suppose we really never know what difficulties others are living with, do we?"

"No, Chrissie, we don't; and we often don't know what's going through our own subconscious mind, either. If we do find out, isolating the cause can be even more difficult. I'm afraid that normal therapy sessions, which tend to be slow, give the subconscious time to work out ways of hiding the truth, which it does by coming up with other explanations. It develops explanations that seem plausible, but are often only a detraction from the truth."

"Why would the subconscious do that? You make our

subconscious minds sound more like the enemy than something that's supposed to be helping us."

"Yes, I suppose I do; but the subconscious plays by a different set of rules, different from the logical mind. It will often withhold information and details of past events, which it thinks might upset you."

"Sneaky, is it?"

"This is just how the subconscious functions. It will often create anger around a problem to protect the sensitive emotions of Love from being hurt. But, Chrissie, Love is the only certain cure. That's why it's so important that the subconscious is not allowed to dominate."

"I've never seen anyone alter so quickly, Malcolm. Jenny was with you for only forty minutes. How did you do it?"

"As I keep telling you, it's called Love. Replace thoughts of unhappiness or anger with Love, and the world about you will change, as well. That doesn't mean we should suppress anger. Rather, we should try to understand our anger—and how it hurts us. We usually need someone to express our emotions through, which is why we shouldn't overreact if a friend gets upset. They're probably using us to work out their anger and frustration."

"That's a bit abstract, Malcolm."

"Not really. If you feel anger towards someone because they have hurt you in some way, they cannot even begin to put it right until you let them have the anger back, so they can dissolve it with Love. After all, it is their anger you feel—they caused it. So feel Love for them, and the anger will go back to the one who caused it."

"What if they don't want it back?" This thought amused Chrissie.

"Then it will remain around them until they do. What's important is that you don't harbor anger because of the actions of another. If you do, it will only make you sick in some way. Remember what I said earlier, Chrissie. If someone tries to annoy you or cause you difficulties, ignore it. They have the problem, not you. Unless, of course, you take the emotion of the other person and react to it. Then you relieve them of their anger, and you have the problem."

"So what happens if I'm angry with myself?" asked Jill. She and other members of the group had settled nearby and were joining in the discussion.

"If you recognize that you're angry with yourself, you're lucky, Jill, because you can at least do something about it. It's tough for those who blame others when the problem lies within themselves. They can't satisfy their anger, and it just goes on and on."

"Can you give us an example?" Jill asked.

I thought for a moment or two, sifting through case histories, before saying, "Ok, let's imagine that your husband left you for someone else four years ago and that you are still full of rage and anger against him, even though you haven't seen him since he left."

Someone behind me added: "I don't think that's unreasonable."

"What? After four years, don't you think you should've gotten over it? ...that you should be getting on with life again? Well, at least you shouldn't be all consumed with anger after that period of time. You didn't cause the situation, so why should you be suffering the consequences of anger?"

"Depends upon the circumstances, surely," Chrissie suggested.

"I don't think so. If someone is still in a rage after four years, there's a deeper problem. For some reason, the anger isn't satisfying the emotion of loss; and damning the husband who left is obviously not dealing with the problem."

A woman who was perched on one of the tree stumps beside me asked: "So what should she do? I have an interest in this discussion because my eldest daughter has a problem just like the one you're describing."

"Well, don't take the story I'm putting together personally, will you. Everybody has reasons for the emotions they have, and all will be different. In the case of the woman I'm discussing, her continued anger was not with her husband at all. It was a reaction to a childhood rejection."

Chrissie reminded me that this was the third rejection trauma I'd talked about. "Childhood rejection certainly causes some problems, doesn't it?"

"Yes. In this case, the child's father was away from home a lot. Let's say he worked on an oil rig, and she saw him only twice a year. She loved her father and lived for the weeks when he was home because he spent most of his time with his little girl."

"Mother's not going to like that!" one of the others added.

"Of course not, and so mother became jealous of the daughter. Mother reacted with anger and frustration—but not while father was home. Her anger surfaced while he was away. Mother blames every difficulty on her daughter because daughter was there and her husband wasn't. Daughter began to feel guilty—mother often expressed her loneliness and said it was her daughter's fault. Over the years, the daughter had to endure the mother's anger and loneliness. Eventually, she got married and left home."

"You should've worn jeans, Chrissie," I heard someone say.

"How was I to know I had sat on an ant hill?" she asked, slapping away at the ants that had been sent to remove a squatter from their property.

"Ok, where did we get to?" I asked, hoping to refocus the discussion.

"Hey! Wait till I'm ready!" Chrissie said, moving to a new position. Once settled, she said, "Ok, I'm ready now. Continue the scenario."

"Right. Our lady, let's call her Beth, is now married, perhaps with a family; and twelve years into the marriage, her husband disappears. So, how do you think her subconscious will react?"

"I know how my logical consciousness would react," Jil volunteered. "I would be furious and sad in one breath."

"Yes, Jill, but the long-term effect will be decided in the subconscious."

"So what does it do?" asked Chrissie. "And, does anyone have anything to put on ant bites? They've very big teeth for such little mouths!"

"I don't think we're particularly interested in where you've been mauled, Chrissie, so cover up before the mosquitoes get a meal, as well," I said, jesting.

Chrissie's frown expressed her annoyance, and she continued to scratch through her skirt. "So what does her subconscious do?"

"The subconscious remembers when Beth was a little girl and how she was treated by her mother, when the man she and her mother loved went away. Again, the man she loves has gone away. Suddenly, all the pent up anger of the injustice she suffered in her childhood years breaks loose. But who can she blame?"

"Her husband," Jill responded, as she passed a bottle of insect repellent to Chrissie.

"That's who she thinks she's blaming; but she's really blaming little Beth—just like her mother did. Of course, she doesn't logically connect her anger to her childhood problems with mother."

I heard several 'Hmms' and sighs as the group tried to explore my reasoning. "She obviously can't blame father," I added for clarification, "she always loved him."

"Right," someone agreed.

"And she can't blame mother, who filled her with guilt and made Beth feel it was all her own fault. So, she turns on herself and blames little Beth."

"Let me get this right," Chrissie said. "Are you saying that Beth is angry with herself?"

"Yes, Chrissie, she's really angry with mother, of course, but can't accept that because of the guilt. So, she blames herself."

"…sounds like a lady who doesn't like herself and doesn't know why," a person sitting behind me suggested.

"That's right," I continued, "and we know that because Beth can't remember anything of her childhood—absolutely nothing."

"How do you help her get free of the anger?" Jill asked.

"She has to be regressed to her childhood and helped to remember exactly what happened. This is the only way for her to recall her childhood rejection and to stop raging at the husband for something that's not his responsibility. She also has to begin to like herself again, and she can do that only when she is able to recall all the events of her past, when she can take little Beth in her arms and tell her how much she loves her."

"You mean like you did with Jenny last week?"

"Yes, that's it, Chrissie."

The picnic had been wonderful, but the sun was setting. People began to leave. Chrissie, who was suffering from the bites on her legs, also decided to go.

"I wish you could heal ant bites," she said, frowning. "I'll phone later in the week to make another appointment. I don't think we've finished this subject yet."

Chapter Eighteen
GUILT

"How is he?" I heard Debbie ask someone at the reception desk.

"Oh...not very good."

I smiled and thought, "That's Chrissie's gift to the world." The sound of her voice could always make a person smile.

"Hi Malcolm!" she said, hesitating at the door. "Can I come in and sit with you for a bit?"

"Sure, but I've got a lot of writing to do. I won't be very attentive."

"That's ok. I just want to sit in the healing energy for a while."

Chrissie selected a chair in the corner and settled herself into it. I continued with my writing—I was deeply involved in my thoughts and didn't want to lose them.

Eventually, I couldn't stand it any longer. "Alright, Chrissie, you win." I laid my pen down and turned to face her.

"Have I done something wrong?" she said, accentuating a mocked look of surprise on her face.

"Oh, come on, Chrissie. The silence you've created is deafening. How can I work with noise like that about me?"

She continued in her silence, so I waited until she found the space in her thoughts to tell me what was on her mind.

"I was just thinking how lucky I am."

Her voice, quiet and introspective, held a volume of gratitude and sadness all mixed up together. "I know," I said. "We all get to that point once in a while, especially when someone we know seems to be managing with problems we think we wouldn't be able to deal with. Who do you have in mind?"

"You know the Jensons, don't you?" she almost whispered the words, as if talking to herself.

"Yes." I waited.

"I was with them yesterday and this morning. They are such a lovely family."

More silence. "And…?" I prompted.

"I was just thinking what a beautiful family they are and realizing how much love flows among them. And, little Ben is a perfect angel."

"How old is he now?"

"Twelve, I think, Malcolm. "Daniel is sixteen, so Ben must be at least twelve."

"So, that means Jackie is about eight, right?"

"I would think so."

Chrissie began to come alive as the conversation started to flow.

"Ok, Chrissie, why are you so thoughtful about them today?"

"I've just left the hospital, and little Ben is very ill. They don't think he will survive."

"Oh, I'm so sorry. I hadn't realized there was a problem."

I was surprised by this news. Usually, Chrissie's friends kept me informed about how their youngest son, Ben, was doing. He had been born with physical difficulties and had suffered all his little life, but the love Ben radiated would light any dark night. He was a beautiful child, and his parents, Yvonne and Tony, absolutely adored him. Ben may not have had as many privileges as other children, but God had blessed him with an abundance of love—his parents added to it with all the love they were.

"Have you known them very long?" Chrissie asked. "Oh, I remember now. They introduced you to me."

"That's right. I guess I've known them for at least five years. I recall that first meeting. I had been asked to call in on them by a friend. They were expecting me; and, like all loving parents do, Yvonne and Tony took me straight to their ailing child. They were so proud of Ben, I recall. While they were telling me all about him, an older body came into the room."

"Oh, this is Daniel, our eldest son," Tony said, introducing Daniel.

"Daniel nervously said, 'Hi,' and then went and sat quietly in the corner. He was shy; and seemingly, he did not want to intrude."

"As I gave healing to Ben, I could see why everyone adored him. He was beautiful. Compared to most children, Ben was very physically disabled—confined to a wheelchair and had to have every natural function attended to for him."

"Do you think you could improve Ben in any way?" Yvonne asked nervously.

"Why on earth would I want to?" I gasped. "He's beautiful and perfect as he is."

Tony looked a bit surprised. So, I turned to him and continued: "Look at it this way, Tony. If I wanted to change Ben in any way, I would have to reject him first. You can't change anyone without first rejecting them as they are, and no one likes to be rejected."

"But we haven't rejected him," said Yvonne. "We want the best for him."

"Of course you haven't," I replied, smiling and drawing Tony and Yvonne to me as I moved out of Ben's hearing range. "A parent's love for her children is a different thing. You love little Ben exactly as he is. You totally accept him, while still wanting the best for him; but if I came in here thinking 'You poor little boy…let's see if we can change this or that,' I would be rejecting Ben as he is."

Their slight nods and facial expressions told me that Tony

and Yvonne were agreeing. "I couldn't possibly do that to such a beautiful child. God has never put imperfect love on the earth. Healing is all about unconditional love, which put another way is unconditional acceptance; and in that total loving acceptance, Ben can change himself if he chooses to."

"I hadn't thought of it that way," Tony said.

"That's a lovely way to think," Yvonne added, beaming. "We do love Ben totally; to us, he is perfect as he is."

"You know, Yvonne, Ben knows he's perfect, too. It's others who seem to equate perfection with their own state of being."

"Your message about unconditional love, total acceptance must have meant a lot to Tony and Yvonne," Chrisse said, encouraging me to continue.

"Yes, I think it did; and just as Yvonne finished talking, a little girl walked in. She was lovely! She appeared to be about three years old; and like all children, she didn't recognize ill health or differences…just love. She was so cute, Chrissie. She walked right over to Ben, ignoring me, and reached up to give him a big hug."

"She is a precious little girl. Ok, Malcolm, what happened next? This is a wonderful story. It's making me feel better."

"As I recall, Yvonne introduced the little girl by saying, 'This is Jackie, our gift from God. We hadn't expected her, but we know God wanted to give us a gift of love to help us through. This is Malcolm, honey. Say hello.' I saw the love in Yvonne's eyes."

"And I see the love in your eyes, as you tell the story, Malcolm," Chrissie injected.

"Who wouldn't love such a beautiful child, Chrissie? Jackie turned to me, looked up with her big, beautiful blue eyes, and said: 'Hi, Malcolm.' Then, she just turned to go the way she had come."

"Her baby eyes were like huge sapphires. Ok, Malcolm, tell me more. Where's this story going? What's the lesson?"

"Tony spoke next, Chrissie, and said: 'Jackie accepted Ben totally.'"

"Why wouldn't she?" I asked him. "Children don't see superiority or advantage: they see just a need for love, which they have no difficulty giving."

We chatted for a little while, and I got ready to leave. As I was going through the door, I turned to Daniel, gave him a wink, and said, "Why don't you come and see me sometime. I'll show you what I do."

"Did he accept your invitation?"

"Yes, he did, Chrissie. Daniel was intrigued by my work, especially when I asked him to hold his hand out so that he could feel the energy."

"You and Daniel are quite close now, aren't you?" Chrissie asked, as my thoughts lingered in the first moments of my acquaintance with Daniel.

"Are you still with me, Malcolm? Hello."

"Sorry, Chrissie. Yes, I really like Daniel. He is as full of love as anyone I've ever met.'

"…has a bit of an attitude though, doesn't he?" Chrissie asked, with a hint of criticism in her voice.

"Perhaps, but you know, Chrissie, Daniel has had the hardest time of any of the family."

Chrissie looked surprised. "Why would that be? He's loved, does well at school, and Yvonne and Tony have always been sure to see that Ben's condition doesn't affect Daniel's life or his fun. They treat him with lots of love and care, too."

I realized that we were getting into a deeper level of awareness and that I would have to be careful how I proceeded. I didn't want Chrissie to misunderstand or have her feelings hurt.

"On one occasion when Daniel came to see me," I began, "he told me how he had felt after Ben had been born."

"How was that?" she asked.

"He remembered how his whole world turned upside down."

"Yes, I suppose it did," Chrissie said, speaking to herself more than to me.

"Up until Ben's birth, Daniel had been the center of attention;

and then, that all changed in one day. The excitement of expecting a little brother to play with suddenly transformed into an atmosphere charged with sadness, grief, and disappointment."

"He must have been very confused," Chrissie commented beginning to think from Daniel's perspective.

"Well, just think about it, Chrissie. For four years, he had been the center of attention, enjoying love and happiness; and then suddenly, the attention was all gone. His parents, instead of being happy and excited, loving and attentive, were frightened and locked into their worries and concerns."

"But Malcolm, Yvonne and Tony would never have just forgotten Daniel."

"Of course not, but he was no longer the center of attention. He was confused and felt rejected. I remember his telling me how he used to lie awake at night worrying for his parents. He didn't know what to do to help them."

"Oh, Malcolm," Chrissie the softie said, catching the first tear that formed in the corner of her eye. "I hadn't thought about it like that."

"You see, Chrissie, Daniel wasn't allowed to help. He was only four, and Ben needed a lot of help that only adults could give.'

"Oh..."

"His parents still loved him deeply, but he was a very sensitive little boy. As the years went by, he began to feel guilty if he took up any time or attention that his little brother needed."

"I never noticed this side of Daniel, Malcolm. Are you sure about his feelings of guilt?"

"Yes, Chrissie, Daniel was one lonely boy—a child who wanted to do so much but who was too small to help, feeling guilty for being in the way. He has never really been allowed to help, and so he developed a guilt complex about being in the way, which is why he now sits so quietly and keeps himself out of the way."

"He isn't always so quiet!" Chrissie retorted. "I don't think you know him as I do. There are times when he shouts and gets angry...has a real attitude problem. Just the other day, someone asked him to do something, and he flew into a rage."

"But is that so unreasonable, Chrissie?"

"Well, I think it is," she replied, looking surprised by my support for Daniel's supposedly unreasonable attitude.

"Oh, come on Chrissie. Stop and think about this for a minute. As a little boy, Daniel was desperate to help his parents in any way he could and was told he wasn't big enough or fast enough. Every time he tired, they gave him some other reason why he wasn't allowed to help. Most of all, he was made to feel like an incompetent little boy; and now, he is shouted at or criticized for not doing enough. He is now expected to take full responsibility."

I hesitated and studied Chrissie's face for a moment. She was in deep thought. "Can't you see that Daniel is still feeling guilty? Earlier, he felt inadequate and unable to help; now, he doesn't know how to switch and assume full responsibility. He still feels inadequate and has deep guilt about not being able to help his brother Ben."

"But I thought he was being unreasonable. He has so much; his brother has so little."

Chrissie was becoming thoughtful. I lowered my voice in order to amplify my concern for Daniel and said: "The fact that he is fit and healthy adds to his guilt, Chrissie. Daniel's only defense is to be aggressive at times, to hold people back from criticizing. Can't you see, inside, Daniel is hurting more than you can imagine; but he has no way of expressing that hurt. He mustn't cry because his parents have enough to worry about, and his guilt complex won't allow him to tell them how he feels. Try to understand, Chrissie. Even when he is sitting quietly, this boy is screaming inside."

"I got it completely wrong," said Chrissie, now allowing her silent tears to roll down her cheeks. "I thought perhaps he was jealous of the attention the others got, because Yvonne and Tony so adore Jackie."

"Well, it certainly doesn't help when they keep telling everyone in front of Daniel that Jackie is their gift from God to help them with Ben."

"Now I understand why he feels guilty."

"The situation was a lot easier for Jackie. She never knew what it was like to be the only child, receiving all the parents' love and attention, and then have it taken away.'

"But, Malcolm, Yvonne and Tony are wonderful, caring parents. They love all three children equally."

"I know that; Daniel knows that," I tried to explain to Chrissie, who was beginning to act a little defensive—defending the friends, and wonderful parents, whom she loved.

"But…"

"What no one seem to have noticed is how lonely, forgotten, and guilty Daniel feels."

Silence swelled in the room for a few seconds as Chrissie considered my comment, eyes down. When she glanced up, I said, "You see, Chrissie, it isn't Jackie who is God's gift to the family. It's Daniel. God knew that Ben would be born one day and so sent Daniel first, a real angel, because only a child with Daniel's love could have coped with the trauma he had to struggle with alone."

Chrissie reached for the familiar tissue box.

"If anything happens to Ben, Chrissie, it will be God's first gift to the family who will hold everything together. Daniel's love surpasses everyone's."

"Thank God for gifts like that," said a weepy-eyed Chrissie.

"The younger ones always seem to be the angels; and too often, the eldest feel forgotten and guilty. They also need lots of love…they are angels, too."

Chapter Nineteen
REINCARNATION

"How are the ant bites, Chrissie?"

"Oh, they've healed, thanks," she replied, smiling. "Can we continue with the topics we were discussing at the picnic?"

"Of course, where do you want to start?"

"Well, Malcolm, I've been thinking about staying free of anger; and my thoughts have led me to a new perspective—most of the anger I feel results from the attempts of others to provoke it in me."

"How do people do that?"

"By complaining, I suppose…complaining about the government, their friends, their jobs. You know what I mean, Malcolm. I suppose that I get involved when I start agreeing, which means I become annoyed. If I disagree, we both become angry."

"It's just best to ignore such complaining."

"But, we can't ignore all of it. People expect us to agree with them or at least have opinions, which, of course, they don't expect to differ from their own."

"Still, Chrissie, I say ignore it. Don't let people infect you with their anger or problems."

"I wish I knew how."

"Well, it's a bit like those times when someone comes up to

you and says, 'You don't look very well. Are you ok?' If you are not on top of the situation, you will instantly feel sick and tired; and the other person will go on their way feeling great. All you have to do is reply with 'I feel fine! It must be you who doesn't feel well.' You will continue to feel great, and the person trying to pass the burden of unhappiness will turn away. They'll try to pass their unhappiness on to someone else. I'm sure you've come across similar situations Chrissie."

"Oh, I have," she replied, laughing, "many times; and such negative suggestions can be surprisingly effective. I especially remember one time when I was feeling really good until someone asked: 'Are you ok? You look tired.' Zip! I went right down and got quite depressed. Next time, I'm going to pass it right back, as you suggested."

"And, do the same with every other negative emotions, Chrissie. Don't accept someone else's baggage. Pass it straight back…doesn't matter whether it's anger, jealousy, or self-pity. Refuse to accept other people's negativity. If they want to be unhappy, that's fine, and their choice; but don't allow anyone to infect you with their unhappiness—even if it means losing friends. Always be true to yourself."

"I suppose that passing my happiness on to others is the best thing to do."

"Yes, always. Just remember, only one emotion is more infectious than happiness. Can you guess?"

"Unhappiness?"

"Right…always refuse it."

"Some people aren't going to like your saying they shouldn't be angry or sad, Malcolm. Some don't want to be happy and want to be mad with someone. They won't want to accept this talk of happiness and love."

"Well, it's about time they started! When people leave this world and make the transition to the next one, they will find that any effort they made in life to be helpful and loving will have decided their fate in the next world. Many people think that all their sins will be forgiven or forgotten when they get to heaven just because they belong to a religion. They believe it isn't important if they are angry, jealous, or negative in some other way provided they belong to their chosen religion. However, our emotions are of paramount importance; they are far more important than the religions we join. To be loving but not a believer is of greater value than being without Love but religious."

"Are you suggesting that religion has no value?"

"No, of course I'm not. Religion teaches, or should teach, about God, Love, and morality. Religion should be about family values, community spirit, and helping the young, the sick, and the elderly; and, of course, it usually is. Religion shouldn't teach superiority, separation of people, or forgiveness of their own and damning others. The everyone-is-wrong-but-me principle is void of Love and causes some people to think that only their religion is acceptable to God."

"But religion is important to people. Isn't it?"

"Of course, Chrissie, we need religions—different religions that reflect different cultural values; but most of all, we need religions that teach us how to Love, to experience humility, and to remove fear from our lives. Yes, we need religions...religions that can teach the beauty of transition from this world to the next."

"I suppose that our religious beliefs do influence our transitions," Chrissie said, obviously in deep, deep thought.

"The spirit world really objects to religions that preach fear, superiority, and possessiveness and give credibility to acts of violence or power, their own power."

"How does our thinking about religion make a difference, Malcolm?"

"When we make the transition from this world to the next, we move into a much finer vibrational energy; and any coarse energy we have created with our thoughts of anger, selfishness, power, etc., will act as a barrier to our movement into the spheres of Light and Love."

"Explain what you mean by finer vibrational energy."

"You see, Chrissie, the next world is far more ordered and disciplined than this one. It's the world of thought...created out of what we think. It determines our life-style, our friends, and our place in the scheme of things."

"Awesome! Tell me, will the angry people be unable to reach the loving?"

"That's right, Chrissie. People who are hateful, angry, or superior—unloving in any way—will be unable to move into the light. We are all drawn into an atmosphere that is in harmony with the way we think. The social order in the spirit world is based on the thoughts we are, not our education, wealth, or power. Therefore, anyone who is mean or hateful will live amongst others who are also mean and hateful, even if these spirits would never have associated in the physical world because of social barriers. Status has no place in the spirit world."

"So, how many places are there in the spirit world, Malcolm?"

"Presently, I am aware of three dark spheres, as they are called, one gray sphere, and seven spheres of light."

"What decides which sphere we go into?" Chrissie asked looking confused.

"The way we think and our readiness to serve and learn."

"What sort of things do we learn there?"

"Well, Chrissie, it all depends on which sphere we prepare ourselves to enter."

"Explain."

"Well, consider, for example, someone who is not really bad, a person who goes to church regularly, works hard, but doesn't do much to help others. This person is not really interested in spiritual Love, community work, or that sort of thing. He or she has a what's-mine-is-mine personality and rationalizes by thinking 'I've worked hard for what I have, and I don't care about anyone else.'"

"Where will this person go in the spiritual spheres?"

"Someone like we've described will go to the gray sphere. It's only gray, of course, to those who are in higher spheres. In the gray sphere, the people are selfish, Chrissie. They're just unconcerned for the welfare of others. In that world, spirits learn to love more completely, to be more aware of the needs of others."

"Do selfish spirits stay in this sphere forever, Malcolm?"

"No, this is one of the spheres that people are reborn from—those who get another opportunity to put previous wrongs right. Many people in this sphere are quite happy to stay as they are. To them, it's a lot easier than going back to Earth and beginning again; but this is what they eventually have to do."

Chrissie was already developing empathy for spirits who reside in the gray sphere. "Don't they get an option?" she asked. "I mean what happened to free will and all that?"

I understood her concern about someone being forced to return to life against their will. "Sometimes they have the option," I assured her; "but some just stay where they are for hundreds of years, as measured by Earth time, neither progressing spiritually nor emotionally."

"I didn't think that we would have emotions on the other side," Chrissie said, looking even more confused.

"Emotions are based on fear or love, Chrissie; and with greater awareness of beauty, Love, and God, we will have fewer emotions of fear. We cannot begin to move into the spiritual spheres of light until we have eliminated all emotions of fear."

"All fears?"

"While on the Earthly plane, there will always be some emotions of fear, of course. It's what protects us from hurt; however, problems arise when a passing emotion becomes stronger than the underlying Love. People go down into the first or second dark spheres when emotions of fear cause personalities such as the hateful, vengeful, jealous, or greedy to develop. The more people are without Love, the darker their spiritual sphere. Love lights our lives."

"I'm confused but fascinated, Malcolm. What about people who were full of Love but, through circumstances beyond their control, lived or died in fear?"

"Good question. Depending upon their Love, they would go to the gray area or into the first sphere of light, which is the first true spiritual sphere. There, they'll be healed of hurt or fear, which others caused them during their Earthly life."

"And be reborn?"

"Perhaps. Once a spirit begins to move up into the spiritual spheres, it will return to physical life only by choice. Spirits select this option only if they want to teach or make available some spiritual message or change in the world."

"Are you saying we come back to Earth from the gray sphere only, Malcolm?"

"Not really because we can come back to Earth from the spheres of Light—but only if we choose to. People have to progress up through the dark spheres and into the gray. We have no choice in the gray, or third dark sphere, Chrissie. If we want to progress, we have to return to Earth, and continue to do so, until we learn how to eliminate the emotions that oppose Love."

"I'm not sure that I understand, Malcolm. If we are likely to get involved in fear and other emotional problems, why do we have to come back? This seems like a waste of time, if we're not going to gain from the experience. Why put ourselves through all the fear, superiority, and possessiveness—pain? We could stay in the spiritual planes and not be exposed to risks or emotions!"

"That's not quite true, Chrissie. In the dark and gray spheres, we are exposed to temptations. We actually come up into the dark spheres from another level altogether and have to progress through it, but I'll come to this later on. For the moment, let's stay with the area from which reincarnation takes place."

"At last! You're going to tell me how it all works." Chrissie was being mischievous, but she had waited many weeks for me to get around to this topic.

"Well, there really isn't much to tell you."

"Wait a minute! After all the suspense and waiting, you have nothing to say! You are a disappointment," she said, smiling widely.

"If you think about it, I've already given you most of the reasons for experiencing physical life. It's to help you progress to a point where you move beyond negative or selfish attitudes. Life is about spiritual progression; and eventually, everyone moves from fear to Love, even if it takes hundreds of lives or thousands of years."

"How are we born again? Do we choose our parents, and..."

"Stop! Slow down, Chrissie. I can answer only one question at a time."

"Sorry...I just want to know how reincarnation works."

"Let's start with parents. When the time comes for us to reenter physical life, we either choose our own parents or have them chosen for us."

"Why can't we choose our own?" she asked immediately.

"Sometimes, we do make the selection, or at least choose from a limited number of suitable situations. One criteria for parents is that they have been associated with us in previous life situations."

"Why's that?"

"Because the previous association makes for easier bonding. The vibrational energies of mother and child will be similar, which gives the child a secure and healthy start in life."

"What if associations in a previous life were not totally positive?"

"Reincarnation really holds your interest. You're full of questions, Chrissie. And, yes, oftentimes, the child needs to work through some emotion with one of the other family members."

"Does the spirit of a person who is reincarnating come to Earth with a completely pure mind, Malcolm? Will it have any emotions to start with, other than the Love it is gifted with?"

"All children start life with their spiritual Love complete, but any emotions from a previous life, which the returning spirit left behind, will be ready and waiting. When the spirit reenters the Earthly vibrational plane, the emotions of the previous life will attach to the physical mind of the child spirit."

Chrissie gasped and then thought deeply before asking, "So no matter what we do, at some point in time we have to come back to deal with the negative emotions we left behind from previous trips."

"Yes, that's right. This is a part of reincarnation. We cannot escape from whatever harm we have done…harm to ourselves, to other people, to our community, or to the planet. At some point, we have to return and dissolve the negative vibrations we created—any vibrations that are out of harmony with Love. We cannot escape this aspect of reincarnation."

"This sounds so absolute."

"It is. If we have a lingering hurt or fear from a past life, such as the one you had, Chrissie, it causes problems until we bring the hurt or fear into logical awareness and deal with it. This is especially true of the emotions we were feeling at the time of our death. Because these emotions were with us as we died, we don't have an opportunity to release them until we are reborn."

"That's exactly what happened to me, isn't it?"

"Yes. Now you really understand why you had all those unexplained anxieties and fears. They were in your emotional field; and from the time you were born, they lingered just beneath the surface of your emotional field. Meeting Byron brought them to the surface, though not into your logical memory; and then, all your old emotions of fear and love surfaced. Do you understand now why you experienced the love, the fear, and the physical hurt. This time, Byron handled the situation better than he did during your previous lives together. You were able to release the fear from your emotional field, making it easier for you to move spiritually into the spheres of light, which is where your creativity originates."

"Does everyone reincarnate with some fear or negative emotion. Surely, Malcolm, I'm not unique."

"Indeed, most everyone does. Rebirth is an opportunity to overcome weaknesses or negative emotions and to let Love take their place. It can be a long, hard journey; but by facing up to our fears and becoming Love, we eventually enter into the first sphere of light, from which there is no need to return."

"When we enter the first sphere of light, do we become angels, saints, or something?" Chrissie asked, laughing, but serious.

"No. This is a question I'm often asked. Our personality doesn't change when we die, but the Love we are becomes more radiant—our lives more contented and happy."

"And people who don't make it into the light…?"

"People who enter the gray sphere are very much as they were on Earth, Chrissie. They are what they think—they become their thoughts. If they still need gold trinkets, for example, they will have them. In fact, they'll have whatever they want. These spirits think they should be as they were on Earth—this seems natural to them. God lets them have what they want, for they are as children with toys, and waits for them to stop wanting. Eventually, they begin to realize that material things are unnecessary and understand that their possessions block the path to Love and happiness."

"You'll have a hard time trying to convince people to give up what they've inherited," Chrissie said, giving me a comforting smile. "Surely you're not going to tell people that they've got to give their possessions away…to prove they are loving?"

"Of course not, Chrissie. Inheriting wealth or creating it during a lifetime isn't wrong. What individuals do with their wealth is the issue. If wealth is used to cause hurt or harm to others, the wealthy will have to put things right in the future. This is also true for those who have a passion for possessions or people. If we value anything above Love—anything for which we have no need but try to keep to ourselves, we will be reborn with the purpose of learning how to go without. When wealth is used sensibly to help others or to create beauty in the lives of people, however, this is an action of Love and builds on the beauty and radiance that awaits our return to the spiritual world."

I could see more questions forming in Chrissie's mind and knew that our discussion of reincarnation was far from finished. She pursed her lips and wrinkled her brow just before asking, "Can people who've stolen in order to be wealthy keep their wealth? What about people who've become rich through drug sales, or corruption?"

"Wealth acquired by such means must be returned; and if people have been hurt by the acquisition of such wealth, the aggressor must make amends, during this lifetime or the next. That's why some people find that money just flows away from them, no matter what they do to control it. This doesn't apply to all cases, of course, but it's often the reason why people cannot manage money effectively. The same reasoning applies to all areas of life."

"Do we have a name for this reasoning?"

"Yes, Chrissie, it's called Karma, which is an Egyptian word. When people mention their Karma, they are referring to the reasons for their rebirth—to correcting any wrongs their spirit did to others in a previous life. Whatever deliberate hurt or harm was committed to an individual, a community, or even to the world of nature must all be put right before the spirit can progress; and sometimes, this takes several lifetimes."

"Most people won't be able to remember what it was they did wrong, so how can they possibly make corrections, Malcolm? I know that I would never have remembered that one particular situation without your help."

"We are deliberately placed in situations where we have the opportunity to correct previous wrongs, even if we aren't consciously aware of the wrongs. Very often, people go on and on, lifetime after lifetime, committing the same mistake, hurting the same people. That's why it's so important to overcome our karma and to become Love."

"Can people overcome their karma? Seems to me that lifetimes could be wasted if we're not told what we're doing wrong."

"People know, Chrissie. It's just that they prefer to ignore their conscience. In their hearts, people know when they are doing something that offends Love. We all know if we are being loving or critical, hurtful or helpful, negative or positive. Making excuses for our actions doesn't get us out of anything. Oftentimes, people turn situations around and claim that someone made them do what they did. I'm always surprised by the many excuses people come up with when they continue to do wrongs—and know in their hearts that they are doing wrong."

"I suppose I've been guilty of this as well, Malcolm. Why do we do it?"

"The problem is that people have come to ignore the inner voice of Love so easily that it doesn't bother them any more, and they can destroy beauty and Love without assuming conscious responsibility."

"That thought makes me feel sad."

"Fortunately, more and more Loving souls are reincarnating; and their task is to create change, to return reason to the purpose of life."

"Everything about life comes back to Love, doesn't it?" Chrissie asked, speaking from her own deep thought world.

Silence fell between us for a few seconds. Both of us were questioning our own purposes for being in physical life, I think. Eventually, Chrissie broke the silence by asking, "Why do little babies sometimes die before they are even born, or soon afterwards, for no apparent reason?"

"You're changing the subject a bit, aren't you? There's always a reason, though. Sometimes we just can't comprehend it at the time."

"Can you explain a situation?" she asked, assuming that I would. "I have a friend who had a miscarriage a few weeks ago, quite late into her pregnancy; and she's heartbroken. I'd like to give her a reason, if there is one."

"Well, I'll try; but until you know more of the workings of the spiritual world, this law may be difficult to understand. When the time comes and the spirit has developed into a true state of Love, has become a spirit of light, it needs an opportunity to grow in a totally loving environment, one free of all emotions except those of Love. This can never be achieved in an Earthly life; and so the spirit for its final journey in a physical profile, begins life as all spirits begin human life by being carried in an Earthly womb. The spirit returns a final time to take to itself the remaining emotions of the Earthly plane. At the right time, the mother's physical body, which the spirit is using, loses its energy and releases the spirit so that it can return as a child spirit and continue its growth in a totally loving and spiritual environment. Of course, Chrissie, the parents grieve the loss of the child. They don't have the wisdom or spiritual insight to know that their love has given refuge to a perfect spirit in readiness for its final journey before it enters the truly spiritual realms of light."

"That's incredible," Chrissie said, as if she were speaking to herself. She was still deep within her own world of thoughts. "The spiritual world uses us and we never know it," she continued. "That doesn't sound very nice, or spiritual."

"Most of what happens to us in a spiritual way, Chrissie, we agreed to before we were born. We just can't remember because we've lost our spiritual perception."

Silence filled the room again before Chrissie asked, "How does a spirit actually become one with a body, Malcolm?"

"...in exactly reverse order as it leaves, I replied. "Do you remember when I told you that we depart life through the center of our emotions?"

"Yes, I do," she said. "You told me that we enter the light as whatever emotion we have allowed ourselves to become."

"That's right."

"...and, we leave behind a sort of fog of emotion, which we have to come back and clear up at some time."

"Yes, Chrissie, your recall is exactly right."

"So, Malcolm, are you saying that we pass out of the light and reenter through the fog of our own prepared emotions, when we reincarnate?"

"Yes."

"...and then blend with those emotions.

"Yes, again."

Thinking aloud, Chrissie nodded and said, "I see. It then becomes a matter of staying with, or becoming one with, the physical. Is this an instant thing, Malcolm, or is some time required?"

"...can take a few weeks or up to seven years, depending on the spiritual nature of the child. Some children resist becoming one with the physical for quite a long time, especially if they are spiritual—if their emotions are of Love and they have had many human lives. These children continue to live in the spirit world as well as the physical for quite some time."

"I have a little cousin who's always talking about a lady she plays with in her bedroom at night. Her parents think she's making it all up; but somehow, I don't think she is. To her, the lady is very real. Is this possible, Malcolm?"

"Lots of children have similar experiences because they live outside of physical reality. Treated with Love, these children grow up to be very loving and spiritual. Unfortunately, they're usually told that they should not talk about such things, or to stop being silly. So, they allow themselves to become totally one with the physical world, and opportunities to learn about spiritual matters are lost."

"Who are the people, the ones children play with, Malcolm?"

"You just asked a complex question."

"Am I about to get a complex answer?" she asked, grinning.

"Yes," I replied, returning her grin. "A question like you just asked has many answers. You see, the lady your little cousin is playing with, although no one else sees her, could be a figment of the child's imagination. Or, she could be a loving relative who is deceased but still watching over the child. As another possibility, the lady could even be the full personality of the child's last life."

"Wow!" Chrissie exclaimed. "Do you mean that my cousin's past emotions can appear to her, as she used to be?"

"...something like that. Most spirit guides, and that's what they are called, are no more than the energy of past-life personalities, which have experience that the spirit needs again. So the spirit, your cousin, calls on the past personality for help. Your little cousin may call upon her past for friendship and security and appear to herself as the happiest of her former personalities."

Chrissie seemed slightly startled by my last remarks. "How can she do that? She doesn't seem special in any way."

"She wouldn't have to be special. She would do it in the same way that you see yourself as a child when you visualize clearly enough. You know how to hold and hug your child, as Jenny did last week. The only difference…a young child can recreate the vision in physical form, using the energy of emotion. We all attract past-life energy to ourselves when it's needed. Anyone who is psychic, anyone who can see energy, will see the images of another's thoughts; and, usually, the psychic believes they have seen a spirit guide, which is most unlikely."

"Lots of psychic people talk about seeing spirit guides, Malcolm; so why do you think that it's unlikely? What are they really seeing?"

"Oh, we are wandering off the subject again; but very quickly, I'll try to explain. A true spirit of Love will have no need to appear as a definite personality, like a Chinaman or a Native American Indian. They are beings of radiant light and beyond even psychic perception. The personalities people see are the thought forms of a past-life personality belonging to the person who is creating them, unless, of course, it's a relative or loved one who has been granted an opportunity to visit someone they love."

"Is that helpful?" Chrissie wanted to know. "Why would someone, especially unintentionally, want to recreate a past personality?

"It can be useful. For example, if someone needs strength or knowledge that is beyond them in the present time, they can call on the energy or knowledge of a previous life; and what they need will be available to them. If the person in our example draws from the energy of a Nordic lifetime, an observing psychic might report the presence of a Viking guide."

"This is too much, Malcolm! Does this mean that my little five-year-old cousin is using her mind to influence the emotional energy of a past life? That she's transforming the energy to an almost solid form?"

"Probably…I can't be sure without more detail; however, children are very spiritual. In the early stages of life, children are often able to utilize past-life energies and emotions, or to see themselves in their previous forms. This is possible because young children are not totally one with their physical bodies. Girls, as they change and become young women, can do the same for periods of weeks or months, which gives rise to the poltergeist phenomena."

"What?"

"No more of this talk, Chrissie. We must get back to the subject. I'll discuss the energies of life another time. So, what were we talking about?"

"…reincarnation. The problem with all of this, Malcolm, is that you can't prove what you've said."

"I know. Since I can't provide evidence, are you going to act against your conscience? Are you going to act as if life ceases the moment a person stops breathing?"

"No. Of course I'm not going to act that way. But, why should I take all of this stuff about reincarnation seriously? There's no proof. No one really knows what happens to us when we die."

"Until you do take it seriously, Chrissie, and begin to live by the spiritual laws of Love, you will continue to reincarnate. Eventually, something inside you will awaken; and then, you'll begin to make the slow journey forward toward the light."

"Something heavy would have to happen to cause a change in most people's thinking, Malcolm. What would cause someone who hadn't been spiritual, to change and become more loving?"

"…usually a terrible catastrophic event. Grief is a great spiritual emotion, and it often helps to move people from selfishness to

Love. Events such as the loss of a loved one, especially a child, or being responsible for an accident can change people. Cancer is often a form of shock therapy that awakens people from spiritual sleep and moves them into awareness of Love. With cancer patients, the way they deal with their last months will make up for much of what was wrong or missing during their lives."

"Seems like some people have to die in order for Love to flourish."

"I'm often asked by parents why the good or loving die young. The answer is simpler than you might think. Death will often awaken the spirit of Love in the living who are left behind, allowing them to grow. Suffering of some form is what usually triggers a move from selfish emotions to Love, Chrissie."

"I want to become Love without having to endure more suffering," she said thoughtfully.

"Never deliberately hurt anyone or allow others to cause you to lose your sense of Love, and the rest will sort itself out."

"Thank you. That's good advice to live by."

Chrissie seemed to withdraw for a moment. I knew she was formulating a question that was deeply important to her and wasn't surprised when she asked, "So, what are your views and thoughts on abortion?"

"As a general principle, I don't approve. Abortion cannot kill a spirit, of course; and provided the procedure is performed before the spirit has become one with the baby and its emotions, which is usually between three and four months, the shock to its little system is limited to one of rejection. But this rationalization doesn't make abortion spiritually right."

"You know that I had an abortion?"

"Yes, you told me earlier."

"But you didn't show any signs of disapproval at the time."

"You didn't ask my opinion, Chrissie; and, anyway, I would never judge any particular situation to be right or wrong without all the facts. Even then, I wouldn't consider what was done in terms of good or bad. It's something you did; and if wrong, the consequences will be worked out at a future date. I accept everyone unconditionally, regardless of what they have or haven't done. To me, what someone is doing or thinking now is of more importance."

"Would you ever tell someone that an abortion is acceptable, Malcolm?"

"No. I would never say that an abortion is the right thing to do, or the wrong thing."

"Why?"

"For one reason, I can't know the right answer. Two separate situations can appear identical; but for subtle differences, one abortion will be the right course and the other wrong."

"Someone must be able to know. Otherwise, we may regress to the belief that all abortions are wrong."

"The only people who can ever know the answer to your questions, Chrissie, are the mother and the unborn child. No one can ever kill a spirit—it's very important that you know this. An abortion prevents a spirit from experiencing life in physical form. If a baby is aborted, at any stage, the spirit returns to the spirit world and waits for a more opportune time to reincarnate."

"How do you advise people about abortion?"

"Several mothers have sought my advice and help. Some have children but are tormented because of having had an abortion earlier in their lives. These mothers have a young family but can't help wondering what became of the child, or children, they rejected through abortion. Often, they aren't able to enjoy the Love of the children they do have because of being so full of guilt, and sometimes grief."

"I can understand," Chrissie replied, speaking softly. Her own emotions were surfacing.

"What they haven't realized, Chrissie," I began with a reassuring tone, "is that the spirit of a child rejected through abortion has probably reincarnated. Most likely, it is alive as the child they gave birth to later."

"Really?"

"Oh yes. Oftentimes, a rejected spirit waits patiently until the time is right and the opportunity arrives for it to be born to the mother of its choice. I have known of the same spirits being aborted two or three times before being reborn."

Chrissie's relief was obvious as she relaxed and slumped into her chair. "I expect these children grow up to be very much against abortion," she said, smiling. "How can you know it's the same spirit? I mean how can you recognize the spirit of a small baby as the same spirit that was rejected earlier?"

"Quite easily!" I replied confidently. "I just take the mother who is worrying into the white light, and she sees the child's spirit, who explains all this to her."

"You mean she just goes into the light and has a friendly discussion with her unborn baby? Oh, come on, Malcolm, does that really happen? Surely it must have something to do with a vivid imagination."

Chrissie was now sitting up straight again and waiting for my response. "It has nothing to do with an overactive imagination, I assure you. Anyone who has experienced such an event has no doubt as to the reality of the experience. Those in the same room as a mother who has entered the white light experience a calm, an atmosphere which is beyond description. This is true spiritual healing...beyond intellectual reasoning or understanding."

She didn't respond. Her questioning eyes told me that she needed more explanation. "I do exactly the same for expectant mothers who are wondering whether they should continue with their pregnancy. They enter the white light and hold in their arms the spirit of the child they are expecting. Only in very exceptional circumstances do expectant mothers reject their baby after they've held and loved its spirit."

"That sounds beautiful. But why would a child decide not to be born?"

"Because, Chrissie, the spirit knows if the situation is not right. At such times, it will agree, or even suggest, that waiting would be better. That is why no one should ever be totally against abortion."

My comment about abortion seemed to comfort Chrissie. Her emotional heaviness lifted. "I've been concerned about how abortion relates to reincarnation," she confessed.

"I do need to stress another point. Decisions to wait are exceptions to the rule. The point I'm trying to make, Chrissie, is that no one other than a mother and her unborn child can know what is right in any particular situation; and I emphasize that no one else is qualified to judge these situations. If a mother meditates or prays in Love and light, without fear, the right answer will come to her."

"But aren't some abortions just simply wrong?"

"If abortions are for selfish or materialistic convenience, then yes, they seem obviously wrong. The unborn child's spirit may feel all the pain of rejection; however, it will still persevere to be born with the mother's next pregnancy. I wouldn't want anyone to use this knowledge as an excuse for an abortion, Chrissie."

"As you've suggested, mothers who have had abortions earlier in life are now probably loving the babies they rejected earlier. Or, rejected spirits are waiting for future pregnancies. If you're right, Malcolm, this information will comfort many women."

"Yes, it should. A spirit cannot be killed by abortion, or any other means. As I've said, life journeys are just delayed; and oftentimes, reincarnation will be with the same parents, or at least in the same family. Once spiritual law has decided that a spirit will be born and the spirit has made its transition from mature spirit to a child spirit, it will not be denied."

"You've given me many thoughts to ponder about reincarnation. People who become aggressive or angry in support of antiabortion beliefs may be upset for the wrong reasons."

"...depends upon what their reasons are. Anger won't solve any problems, Chrissie. Some people have a deep fear of abortion and are releasing their fear as anger. However, that is not the way to deal with it; and someday, they will have to deal with the fear instead of trying to release it as aggression and anger. A better choice would be to express their views through Love, which really causes change."

"A spiritual perspective definitely seems advantageous to all concerned."

"For or against abortion, the first consideration must always be the connection between the mother and the baby, not one or the other. Very occasionally, it's better to defer a birth; and anyway, how can a person other than the mother and the unborn child possibly know what the answer should be?"

"Very good point, Malcolm. I'm glad we've had this talk."

"People who prevent a pregnancy from progressing for reasons of selfish desire will have to make amends at some later time, as will those who knowingly provide the means for rejecting unwanted babies as a way of making money."

"So, the reasons behind the actions are the important considerations?"

"If the reasons are of Love, the decisions will be the right ones."

"And Love never expresses itself as anger or aggression, right?"

"That's right, Chrissie, never."

Chapter Twenty
FEAR

"Malcolm," Chrissie said, sounding hesitant.

"Yes, Chrissie, what is it?"

"Well, I know someone who would like to have an appointment with you, but he's not sure if you will see him."

"Why wouldn't I want to see him?"

"He's a racist and doesn't know how you feel about that sort of thing."

"Everybody knows my views, Chrissie. I accept all people equally, irrespective of their race or religious beliefs. If a person doesn't like me because of my skin color, my religious beliefs, or my life-style, it's their problem, not mine. I'm quite happy being me, and I have no difficulty helping people who find it difficult to accept me. I'm certainly not going to get upset by your friend's racist views. I've never refused to see anyone."

"No, Malcolm," she said, smiling. "This has nothing to do with you. It's just that he has a thing about black people and wondered if you might refuse to see him because of his extreme views."

"Of course I'll see him, Chrissie. To my way of thinking, he has a bigger problem than those he's opposing."

Chrissie smiled again and relaxed. "I knew you would," she said. "He's outside. Can I bring him in now?"

"That's a bit sudden, isn't it? I thought you meant that I would see him next week."

"Oh, come on, Malcolm. You can talk to me some other time; and anyway, he won't come back if we give him time to think about it."

I couldn't conceal my smile. I knew when I was beaten. I really didn't mind, of course, after I realized that Chrissie had manipulated this situation in her usual charming way.

"Ok, Chrissie. How well do you know him?"

"I've know him only a few days. We met at a party, and he was going on about some black guy who was there. His remarks were really racist. Fortunately, the black guy had enough character to ignore the remarks; but this man really has a problem. That's why I suggested that he talk about it with you."

"And he agreed?"

"Yes," she replied, looking a bit surprised. She hadn't expected me to ask the question.

"Chrissie, you should have been a saleswoman. I think you could talk anybody into anything. You're incredible! Ok, what's his name?"

"Todd, Todd Breet."

Chrissie went out and returned with Todd a few minutes later. My first impression of Todd was positive. He appeared to be pleasant, around twenty-three, smartly dressed, and aware of his own importance. He didn't wait for Chrissie to introduce him—he came straight across the room, shook my hand, and introduced himself. Chrissie, who hadn't followed him into the room, discretely returned to the waiting room and began to chat with Debbie.

Todd deliberately left the door open and obviously expected me to go across and close it after him. "This is a young man full of his own importance," I thought to myself. I began to draw on my experience immediately. If I moved from behind my desk to close the door, he would take my movement as a signal that he was the dominant character; and any value in the ensuing consultation would be wasted. I knew that people with his sort of personality have a fear of failure; and if they see what they think is weakness in someone, they immediately move to dominate the situation. They'll dismiss whatever they hear as irrelevant rubbish; and, of course, closing the door for him would have been interpreted as weakness."

So, the door remained open. Todd obviously wasn't going to close it; he waited to see what I would do. "Perhaps you should shut the door. Otherwise, our discussion won't be very confidential, will it?" I suggested.

Todd, who had seated himself opposite me, shrugged his shoulders.

"Well," I continued, "if you don't mind, I don't."

Todd hesitated for a moment; but when he realized that I wasn't going to do anything about the door, he got up and closed it. "Now, we're ready to have a meaningful discussion," I assured myself.

After closing the door, Todd began to tell me about himself. He was born into a very successful family. His father was a well-known banker, all three of his uncles had achieved prominent positions in the military, and a cousin was president of a multimillion dollar corporation. Todd had selected a career in finance and the general assumption was that he would be as successful as the other male members of his family. In spite of his outward display of confidence, I sensed an overwhelming fear of failure in Todd, which he tried to hide behind a disposition of arrogance one moment and charm the next.

This type of personality is often intolerant of others. They interpret any sort of failure as weakness; and because they fear it in themselves, they fear it in others as well. People with this personality come to despise anyone who, in their opinion, has failed or is weak. They dare not associate with anyone who is perceived as a failure or weak in any way.

Early in our conversation, Todd's comments revealed that he was obviously a hypochondriac. This is not unusual in power-motivated people, especially those who unconsciously use a fear of failure as their main driving force. They need something to use as an excuse should things go wrong; and sooner or later, things do go wrong—that's when people with Todd's personality have some illness or other ready as a handy excuse.

This doesn't mean, of course, that they are making it all up. They really do worry about their heart, their stomach, and any other bits and pieces that may give them an ache or two. Problems that most people would brush aside are major areas of concern to this worldly type of personality, and Todd had been perfectly typecast for the role he was about to play in life.

Eventually, I led him into a discussion on race; and very quickly, he let me know how he felt about coloreds, as he put it. In his opinion, black people were somehow less than equal, less than capable of achieving the expectations of the human race. I allowed him to express his views for a while. Eventually, he stressed that his main point was 'worthiness' or lack of it.

Also, Todd's underlying fear of black people became apparent to me. Of course, he would never have admitted this, even if he realized it; but his fear was obvious. In addition to his fear of personal failure, Todd was suffering from some form of fear of rejection and was reacting to it by rejecting an entire race of people.

"Why do you think you feel the way you do?" I asked him.

Todd was honest enough to admit that he had never really thought about his feelings about black people.

"Have you ever been hurt by a black person?"

After a few moments of silence, he admitted that he hadn't. "It's just that they make me feel uncomfortable," he added. "I don't know what it is; but whenever a black person comes into the room, I start to get mad. All sorts of emotions rise up inside of me. Black people always affect me this way. I just wish they would disappear…go away…anything. I just want them to stay away from me."

"Alright, Todd, let's find out where this fear comes from."

"It's not fear!" he replied, nearly shouting. "I just don't like them!"

"That's quite obvious, Todd. Let's see why."

Todd agreed to the healing; but because of his deep subconscious fear, there was a lot of emotional resistance, which took me some time to overcome. Resistance is easily recognized by a build up of temperature between the healer and the client. The healer gets hotter and hotter, as the energy builds, until the emotions of the one being treated are unable to resist the healing energy any longer. Then, as the resistance breaks, the energy transfers from the healer to the client.

After fifteen minutes, Todd's resistance weakened, his breathing quickened, and his heart began to race. He showed all the signs of extreme anxiety. "What's happening to you, Todd?"

"I don't know," he replied, in a voice so low I could hardly hear it.

"What do you see?"

"I don't know," he repeated. "It's too dark to see; I don't feel safe. I don't know why I feel so insecure."

"Are you sitting down or standing up?"

"Oh, I'm sitting, but I can't move. There are people on both sides of me. I'm scared; I feel trapped; and I can't move. I'm trapped in a cave or something."

"Why can't you move, Todd?" I asked, knowing that he was moving into a healing state.

After a few moments of silence, he let out a cry and shouted, "I'm chained! I'm chained! Oh, no," he groaned. "I can't move; it's terrible. There are bodies all around me. I feel crushed. I can't breath properly. The air, it stinks; and my feet are in water."

Todd was now visibly shaking with fear. Sweat was running down his face, and he was rigid in the chair. "What are you sitting on?" I asked.

"A wooden seat or bench. I can't lean back or forward without touching someone." He began to cry. "We're all chained in."

"What are you chained to, Todd?"

Again, he was silent for a few minutes; and then, he let out a long, painful cry. "I'm deep in the hull of a boat. I'm a captive. Oh it's terrible; there are so many of us. Everyone is so silent—no one is making a sound. I can hear the sea pounding against the hull of the boat and people moving about on the upper deck; but in here it's so quiet. Oh, my God! What's happening to me? It's so quiet—no one is saying anything. I feel so wretched, empty inside, and totally beaten."

"Look at your hands, Todd. What color are they?"

Silence filled the room as Todd's facial muscles tightened and perspiration beads formed on his brow. "They're black! I'm a slave!"

Todd began to sob, and the fear that had been reasonably well contained, up until this moment, welled up and broke loose in one long, drawn-out scream, which seemed to go on and on. When he had settled down a little, he started to shake and tremble. At first, I thought it was unreleased fear; but he eventually told me that he was cold.

"I'm cold…so cold," he moaned.

I watched Todd's body shake with cold as he relived his past-life experience, and his teeth chattered as well. All the while, he kept his feet together and sat bolt upright in the chair with his hands to his sides. Occasionally, he swayed to and fro. I assumed that he was experiencing the swell of the ocean and the rocking of the boat.

"It's so quiet…so quiet," he said repeatedly. "No one makes a sound. We are men—not animals."

Todd went on to describe the barbaric treatment he and the others endured until they were led out onto the deck. At this point, the main focus in Todd's mind was the sunlight. He couldn't open his eyes because of the brightness of the sun, after being in the hold in almost total darkness. He was aware of being pushed, beaten, and pulled along. He couldn't see properly. His ankles were sore from the fetters, but his hands were free to steady himself.

Todd continued his story until the day when he was sold into slavery. It was the sad story of a once proud man who'd been stripped of his dignity, self-respect, and confidence. He was made very aware of his color during his past life, and his loss of dignity became synonymous with the color of his skin. Todd was full of fear because of his previous color.

During the life he described, Todd came to fear his dark skin. His color singled him out for harsh treatment in a land and culture he didn't understand. He knew that he was a slave because of his color, not his birth or his culture. He had lost his dignity and position in life because of his dark skin. In his present life, Todd had a fear of failure; and somehow, at a deep emotional level, he knew that dark skin could cause his downfall. For this reason, he became anxious near black people because their presence heightened his emotions of fear. However, the reason for his anxieties were completely hidden from him; and his dislike for black people bordered on hatred.

At the conclusion of the regression, Todd went to the day he died. He described himself as not old but worn, exhausted, and terrified. He was terrified because he was too ill to get up and work. Todd died in fear of being black.

For nearly an hour, Todd relived the emotions and memories of a life he had once endured as a black American slave. At the end, when he had fully recovered his composure, he quietly told me, "I've never known fear like that. It was all so inhuman—degrading. If I hadn't experienced it, I wouldn't have believed this story. At first, I thought I was making it up; but the visions and the emotions I had were so real. I couldn't imagine such a story—it had to come from deep within me."

"So why do you think you are so against black people in this life, Todd? Wouldn't it make more sense for you to appreciate the prejudices and difficulties they have to deal with because of people with views like yours, instead of raging against them as you do?"

Todd sat in silence for a few moments before saying, "You know, Malcolm, I think it's because colored people remind me of the fear I experienced in that life…that's why I try to stay away from them."

He paused and thought before volunteering, "The way my heart pounded and the emotions I felt as I went into the experiences of that life were similar to the way I feel when a black person comes near me. I've got a lot to learn."

I let him continue. He was beginning to realize for himself the reason for his prejudice and racist attitudes. "It's because black people remind me of a life that was full of fear," he said, beginning to smile again. "Wow! My heritage is part African, as well as being white. I can't separate myself, can I, Malcolm? This is confusing. What am I? Black people are part of me; I'm part of them. That thought will take some getting used to."

Todd gave me a half grin. "I can't wait to see my parents' faces when I tell them that I'm of African ancestry. Gee, Malcolm, do you think that the black guys out there were European at some time?"

"Yes, Todd, I do. During their past lives, most men and women on Earth have been every color and every religion and have lived in a variety of cultures."

"Do other people go through the sort of experiences I've just been through?"

"Yes, Todd, but most cases aren't as dramatic as yours. However, I remember a man who really disliked Jews until he regressed to a past life in England when he was a Jewish woman. The woman and her children were killed in York by a religious mob. That experience created a great sense of fear and injustice about Jews; but as he was born Christian in this life, the fear was about Jews, not as a Jew."

"I had no idea that fear could result from previous lives."

"I could give you many similar accounts, Todd. I especially remember a lady who regressed to a life in Ireland and discovered that she had been an Irish Catholic. After the healing, she told me that prior to the regression she had disliked both Ireland and Catholics. She disliked them in this life because she had been badly treated during a previous life."

"I feel better knowing that I'm not the only one who's been guilty of such thoughts and behaviors."

"Unfortunately, Todd, people's feelings don't always come across as just dislikes—sometimes they surface as hate. Your subconscious protects you from fear with thoughts of anger. In cases like yours, that's why it's so important to see life from the other point of view. Every case is different, of course; and I don't mean to imply that people always have dislikes resulting from previous lives. Some people change religions in this life in order to be as they once were, and some go even further and have sex changes. But, skin color cannot be changed."

"The fear I felt was awesome. I'll never forget it."

"In this life, Todd, we tend to dislike and oppose that which caused us fear in an earlier life. Not all of our attitudes or emotions are developed because of our present culture. If we have been oppressed in some way because of race, religion, gender, or any other reasons, we build fear into our subconscious; and to protect us from that fear, like your fear of dark skin, the subconscious causes us to attack that which previously caused us fear. In other words, we attack the life that hurt us."

"That's incredible, Malcolm. This healing has added another dimension to my thinking. I can't possibly be the person I was two hours ago."

"I'm sure you will become a little more tolerant of Africans, and other people who are different from you. I wish that I could get this across to all people with bigoted or prejudiced views…that they're probably hurting the very people they once were in a previous life."

"Have you been of other races, or believed in other religions, Malcolm?"

"Oh, yes. That's why I don't favor any one religion now—I've tried them all. I've also been all colors and have lived on all continents at different times. So I feel equally as comfortable living amongst Muslims or Hindus, which I did for a short time when I was in Africa, as I do living with Christians, or any other people. Humans really are one big family, Todd, playing musical chairs with religion, race, gender, and a whole variety of other socially dividing qualities. We will have learned from our own experiences only when we can accept all people as equals."

"As I just learned from mine."

"As I often say to people, Todd, the religion, race, or culture you dislike today, you were yesterday and will probably be tomorrow."

Chapter Twenty-One
AND FINALLY

"Am I busy today, Debbie?"

"I think you may be," she replied, giving me one of her knowing looks.

"Alright, what's that supposed to mean?"

"You've got Chrissie coming in after lunch; and nowadays, I'm never sure whether it's Chrissie or Chrissie and a friend."

"Ok, Debbie, what do your instincts tell you today?"

"I think she's going to bring a friend. She asked me the same question you just asked."

"Which was?"

"Is he busy today? It's just the way she asks, Malcolm."

Debbie was right; Chrissie brought a friend with her, whom I hadn't met before. The friend was a bit older than Chrissie. "A motherly type," I thought to myself, "perhaps Chrissie has found a steadying influence in life, at last."

"Hi, Malcolm," Chrissie began, "meet Fiona. She's been wanting to meet you for a long time. Do you remember? I asked if I could bring her a few weeks ago. She's got a phobia. Haven't you?" she asked, turning to Fiona, who nodded and tried to mask her embarrassment. "She says I can stay here while you help her with it."

"Hi, Fiona. I want you to sit here," I said, indicating a chair with a straight back. "And, Chrissie, you can sit quietly in the corner."

"So what's the phobia, Fiona?"

She laughed before saying, "I feel embarrassed even telling you about it."

Fiona was about forty, I guessed, and was dressed as if she had come straight from the garden. She was wearing a flower in her hair, a scarf around her neck, and old, heavy work shoes. "This is definitely an outdoor girl," I thought.

"You've never been embarrassed about anything in your life," Chrissie chipped in. "Malcolm, Fiona has a fear of mice. She's as scared of them as anyone I've ever seen. The other day, she found a mouse in the garden shed; and you would have thought she was being tortured. I heard her scream three houses away."

"How long have you been afraid of mice, Fiona?"

"Oh, since I was a little girl. I know what it is, of course."

"You do?" I asked, smiling. "So, what is it?"

People with phobias often think they know the cause of their problem. In reality, however, they know what it is that triggers a fear, which is already lying in wait for someone to awaken it into a phobia.

"Oh, it comes from my mother—she was terrified of mice for some reason. I can remember her getting into a panic when I was very little. She used to completely lose control. So, I expect it comes from her."

"Well, let's find out."

I asked Fiona to close her eyes while I stood behind her; and within a few minutes, she was in a relaxed healing state. I then asked her to go back to the cause of her phobia, to whatever it was or whenever it was. This is the point at which I find out if my client's awareness is going to stay with the current life or regress to a past life. Fiona didn't do either. She was relaxed, but she wasn't releasing any emotion at all.

After a while, she recounted the circumstances of a few instances when she had been embarrassed by her phobia, including the time she ran screaming into another room when a nephew brought his pet mouse to show her.

Then, I asked her to recall the first time she was frightened by a mouse. After a few moments of deep thought, Fiona told me about the time her mother went into a panic because she saw a mouse sitting behind a cupboard in the kitchen. For the first time during our session, she began to show signs of nervousness. I noticed some anxiety in her voice as she described her mother's emotions and reactions to seeing the mouse in the kitchen.

"I was about four or five, I think," she began, sounding cautious. "Mom completely lost control. I'd never seen her like that. She screamed, grabbed a brush, and ran about beating the wall and the cupboard. Mom acted like a crazy woman. I was really scared!"

"Did you see the mouse, Fiona?"

"No, I don't think so. I couldn't understand why Mom was acting that way. I know I was really scared...the way she was screaming at the cupboard. I didn't realize until later that a mouse had caused the panic."

"What did you do while your mother was screaming?"

"I just froze at first...didn't know what to do. She kept on screaming about a mouse; and I think that I began to panic, as well. I suddenly ran out of the kitchen, into another room, and hid under the cushions of one of the chairs."

"What happened then?"

"Dad came in from the garage, and Mom quieted down. I suppose that Dad did something about the mouse. I can't remember that part, but I can still see Mom in the kitchen screaming about a mouse."

"Ok, Fiona, in your imagination, go back into the kitchen. Ignore your mother and look at the mouse behind the cupboard. Can you do that?"

"Yes," Fiona said, attempting to smile. "It's got a pink, pointed nose."

"Does it bother you or scare you?"

"No, not at all."

"Ok, continue to ignore your mother. Now, put your hand out and let the mouse run into it."

Fiona accepted the suggestion and held her hand out. Still quite relaxed and smiling, she held the imaginary mouse in her hand.

"Now, Fiona," I prompted, "take the mouse outside and let the poor little thing go free in the garden. When you've done that, open your eyes."

"I would never have thought that possible," she said a few minutes later, eyes wide open. "I didn't think I could hold a mouse, even in my thoughts."

"The problem lies with your mother, Fiona, not the mouse. What really terrified you was your mother's loss of control. To a little girl, or boy, the situation you described would be terrifying. Parents are supposed to be able to handle every situation; and when they show fear in front of a child, the child picks up the fear and blames the object of the fear. In this case, it was a mouse—instead of the fear itself."

"So what's been happening when I panic over mice?" she asked.

"Mice have reminded you of the time your mother lost control—that's all. You aren't afraid of mice; you've never been afraid of mice. They simply remind you of your mother's behavior, which terrified you. Now that you've realized the connection, you won't fear mice ever again."

"But why do I always run away and hide, Malcolm?"

"Because that's what you did the first time you saw your mother panic. Your subconscious was just reacting to the events of the first time you watched your mother lose control. Mice triggered the reaction, but now that you understand, all of this won't happen again."

"I know you're right, Malcolm; and somehow, I just can't wait to see a real mouse. You know, just so I can prove it."

"It's not unusual, Fiona, for children to have phobias, or even allergies, about things that parents were frightened of in front of them. What they don't realize, however, is that the parent's fear causes the phobia."

"Is that it?" Chrissie asked emphatically, making her presence known.

"Well, what else do you want?"

"But it's only taken fifteen minutes. I thought it would take forever to beat a fear that strong."

"No, Chrissie. Problems like Fiona's phobia can be dealt with quickly. So, what other problems do you want sorted?"

"Malcolm, I have a question about grief."

"Let's have it."

"Ok. Assume someone has died. Would I stop them from going into the light if I kept yearning for them and praying for them to come back, and all that? This is what I've read and been told."

"But what do you think, Chrissie?"

"I'm actually thinking about a friend who has a terrible guilt complex about this. She lost her husband a few years ago and still yearns for him. She misses him terribly, even after all these years; but someone has told her that she is holding up his spiritual progression by keeping him close to her with yearning."

"And?"

"Well, she says she can feel his presence at times; and, sometimes, he answers her thoughts. Is she doing him harm by holding him to her with her love?"

"No, of course not, Chrissie."

"Think about it for a minute. You and Byron are still quite close, right?"

"Yes."

"And you sometimes anticipate his phone calls? You know he's on the line before you answer the phone."

"Oh, I know what you mean," Fiona chimed in.

"My mother and I are very close, and I always know when she isn't well. I can feel it; and when I check on her, I'm right. I phone her when I think she's thinking of me; and when I'm not well, Mother knows and phones me. I have that sort of relationship with several people I know."

"So do you think that someone in the spiritual world is any less able to receive your thoughts?"

"No, I don't suppose so," Chrissie replied.

"Of course not," I agreed. "Thought transference is what communication is all about in the spirit world. Especially if you have a vision of a spirit person in your mind. If you love someone who has passed over, they will receive your thoughts; and you will receive theirs sometimes. As the emotion attached to the memory weakens over months or years, so you will be less able to pick up on their love energy."

Chrissie still wasn't sure. "What about being aware of their presence?" she asked.

"Yes, a person in spirit will stay close for a while, Chrissie; but eventually, if they want to, they go through into the light. However, they can return again once they've become settled in their new world, if the masters who control that world agree."

"So, people here who still love people who've departed aren't doing them any harm by loving them, yearning for them?"

"No, Chrissie. Do you think the world of spirit has less free will than people have here. Those who have passed over can choose for themselves whether they stop or pass straight over. Most do pass straight over; and by the time they're sufficiently experienced to maneuver in their new world, the ones they've left will have lost their sensitivity for perceiving spiritual energy."

"Oh, I see," Chrissie said.

"Don't you think that people waste a lot of time with all that useless yearning, Malcolm?" Fiona asked thoughtfully.

"Yes, they do. If we surround ourselves with physical

reminders of the deceased, so we won't forget them, we cover our lives with the thick emotional fog I'm always talking about. This will do nothing for the ones who have died. They're probably quite unaware of what we're doing because they are getting on with their own spiritual progression. The ones who do all of the yearning and grieving on the Earth side are just building problems for their next lives, both in the spiritual world and here."

"That's easy to say," Chrissie said, turning to Fiona, "but you didn't like being told that at the time you were grieving, did you? It's just not as easy at the time, you know."

"I suppose so," Fiona agreed. "I do wish, however, that someone had told me that my husband was still alive in spirit, after his physical death, and that he could see me and knew each time I cried. It might have been easier to accept that he had left me. If I'd truly known that he was alive in spirit, I wouldn't have kept saying, 'He was a good man' or 'We loved each other.'" Now, I understand that he *is* a good man and that we still love each other."

"Just think, Chrissie," Fiona continued, "I wasted several years of this life grieving because no one had ever explained to me what happens when we die. If people who have lost someone would talk about them as if they're still alive, instead of dead, the feelings of grief would pass much faster."

"Malcolm," Chrissie said, getting up abruptly, "I think we really do need to know more about what goes on in the next world. Can we start to discuss this at our next meeting?"

"And can I come?" Fiona asked.

"Yes," Chrissie answered quickly, smiling smugly. I think I'm going to need some help with the next questions."

"Ok, when I return from my holiday vacation, we'll start with what happens to us when we enter the spiritual world…how our world looks from the other side."

"You're on!" Chrissie said. "Have a great holiday, Malcolm. We'll be waiting."

I watched as Chrissie and Fiona left the office. They were

talking and giggling like two playful children. I had no doubt...they would be waiting.

POPULAR WORKS BY MALCOLM S. SOUTHWOOD

Books

The Healing Experience. Anyone who is interested in learning about spiritual healing will want to read this book more than once. Mr. Southwood shares what he has learned as a full-time healing practitioner and presents many case histories of spiritual healing.

The Challenge. Are we merely the helpless victims of suffering, confusion, and a capricious fate? In this book, Mr. Southwood argues that, on the contrary, each of us possesses, through the energy vibrations of thought, the key to our own well-being, to healing ourselves and others, and to comprehending the nature of existence.

The Ten Great Laws. In this booklet, Mr. Southwood reinterprets The Ten Commandments for practical use in the present age.

Audio Cassette Tapes

In My Silence, Tape One. Dedicated to those going through difficult times; it is softly spoken to comfort and guide you into your silence, where all things are known.

Spiritual Healing, Tape Two. A soothing tape that logically explains healing and how to use it in everyday life.

The Impact of Love, Tape Three. This is a very popular tape. Mr. Southwood shares messages about healing through unconditional love and guides the listener through healing exercises.

The Ten Great Laws, Tape Four. Mr. Southwood reinterprets the Biblical sacred laws as they relate to our present world.

To order
Telephone: 1 610 399-5108
or
Fax: 1 610 399-5109